THE POVERTY OF NATIONS

The Poverty of Nations

A. M. Khusro
Chairman of the Finance Commission
Government of India

Emeritus Professor of Economics
Delhi University

and

Chairman
Institute of Economic Growth
Delhi

First published in Great Britain 1999 by
MACMILLAN PRESS LTD
Houndmills, Basingstoke, Hampshire RG21 6XS and London
Companies and representatives throughout the world

A catalogue record for this book is available from the British Library.

ISBN 0–333–75061–6

First published in the United States of America 1999 by
ST. MARTIN'S PRESS, INC.,
Scholarly and Reference Division,
175 Fifth Avenue, New York, N.Y. 10010

ISBN 0–312–22174–6

Library of Congress Cataloging-in-Publication Data
Khusro, Ali Mohammed.
The poverty of nations / A.M. Khusro.
p.   cm.
Includes bibliographical references and index.
ISBN 0–312–22174–6 (cloth)
1. Poor.   2. Poverty.   3. Poverty—Government policy.
HC79.P6K48   1999
362.5—dc21   99–17494
                                                                              CIP

This book is printed on paper suitable for recycling and made from fully managed and sustained forest sources.

10   9   8   7   6   5   4   3   2   1
08   07   06   05   04   03   02   01   00   99

Printed and bound in Great Britain by
Antony Rowe Ltd, Chippenham, Wiltshire

Contents

List of Tables and Figures

TABLES

FIGURES

Preface

The Economic and Scientific Research Foundation (ESRF) gave me a singular opportunity to address an area of research which has been close to my heart for a long time, when it enabled me to undertake a study of poverty across the international frontiers. For many years I have held strongly the hypothesis that while affluence is growing nearly everywhere in the world, no area of the globe is free of poverty, including some of the most affluent countries and regions. I also hypothesized that in many areas new poverty may be emerging even as old poverty is being conquered. The reason for such beliefs was the continuation of the phenomenon of under-development and the lack of will on the part of governments and peoples of several regions of Africa, Asia and Latin America – the 'third world' – to fight poverty; the failure of the former Soviet Union and allied states in the 'second world' finally to annihilate unemployment, poverty and human distress, especially in the transition from one economic system to another; and the emergence of repeated recessions in North America, Western Europe, Japan and Australia – the 'first world' – which are causing a recurrence of unemployment and human distress in varied forms, from drugs to drunkenness and from new diseases to terrorism.

With encouragement from the patrons of the ESRF and with effective assistance from colleagues, I was able to analyse the phenomenon of poverty in 24 countries of the world, divided into five categories, through five different ways of measurement and at two different points of time. The availability of a vast volume of data in the Human Development Reports of the UNDP, the World Development Reports of the World Bank and several other sources, as well as the evolution of new techniques of measuring poverty like the Human Development Index (HDI), opened up new possibilities of analysis and I was the beneficiary of all these sources.

Suggestions from Dr Charat Ram encouraged me greatly and it was his advice that led me to prepare a special chapter on India. Mr K.K. Podar, Mr R.V. Kanoria, Dr Amit Mitra and Mr M.L. Nandrajog, were always supportive of this project. Collegial discussions with Mr D.N. Patodia and constant advice from him gave a boost to my morale and a fillip to my work. I cannot thank the above-named friends sufficiently for their advice and support. The facilities given by the Federation of Indian Chambers of Commerce and Industry (FICCI) as well as the ESRF efficiently lubricated the research set-up and provided a wholesome atmosphere for work.

But this work would not be what it is without the constant and disciplined encouragement of my economist colleague, Dr M.M. Ansari, and the computer assistance and multi-faceted help of Mr Suresh Mathur, both of whom worked with great sincerity and technical efficiency to complete this research project on the *Poverty of Nations*. I must give my grateful regards to both of them as well as to Mr S. Hajra of the ESRF who kept me free from the details of administration and accounts in this venture so that I could concentrate on the research project without distraction. Mrs Jyoti Ramesh assisted me in the early stages of this project and collected useful information for initiating the research work.

A.M. Khusro

Executive Summary

As the world stands on the threshold of the twenty-first century, terrible poverty still appears to be a universal phenomenon. While most countries and regimes of the world are experiencing an improvement in affluence in varying degrees, the existence of poverty in almost every region cannot be denied. This hypothesis about a simultaneous existence of poverty and affluence everywhere, however, needs to be tested and either established or rejected – wholly or partly – and strategies and policies must be evolved for eliminating the remaining poverty.

In pre-industrial societies, the population-resource balance continued for centuries in several regions and mass poverty did not arise; but feudal and hierarchical social structures spelled socio-economic inequality which became a drag on further growth and development. In addition, many societies suffered from a vicious circle of poverty, a phenomenon which helps to explain the persistence and even the proliferation of poverty, along with many other socio-economic and political factors.

The impact of colonial domination in Asia, Africa and Latin America, mostly by European powers, seems to have caused two opposite effects on the poverty phenomenon in these continents. On the one hand, the colonial powers extensively exploited the resources and siphoned off huge resources to their home countries; but, on the other hand, in order to facilitate this resource transfer, they laid substantial infrastructures such as roadways, railways, ports and communication networks and installed education and health services which, in turn, provided some employment and earning opportunities in the colonies as well as in the home countries. But, in general, it was the former phenomenon of domination and exploitation that led to massive exploitation and expansion of poverty in colonized areas.

Of the many factors that cause economic growth, the major factors, mostly unpredictable and often accidental, are the discovery of mineral wealth or major sources of water, the emergence of technological innovations for the effective exploitation of resources, and the immigration of resilient sections of populations from areas of economic saturation and decline to greener pastures of potential prosperity. Here, these migrated groups apply their resilience and begin the process of taking off into economic growth, which, in turn, provides larger incomes, savings and investments and facilitates poverty reduction.

Yet another factor which stimulates and sometimes initiates economic growth and poverty reduction is the emergence of dynamic leadership which guides societies towards saving, investment, work and high productivity. The leadership and initiatives of Calvin and Luther and the resultant phenomenon of Protestant ethics is a telling example. Conversely, the lack of leadership in many societies has contributed to the persistence of poverty and a continuation of stagnation.

ADVENT OF A MARKET ECONOMY

The idea of a market economy is attributable in the main to Adam Smith, who formulated a new structure of thought which brushed aside the interventionist and semi-controlled regimes of the pre-industrial revolutionary era and laid down the principles of competitiveness, free trade and a freely organized market situation. As the economies of the seventeenth and eighteenth centuries were riddled with intervention, controls and lack of mobility and could not deal with the problem of poverty, the proposition of free trade, free markets and competitiveness, was widely welcomed. It was expected to pull societies out of the depths of poverty and bring about the greatest good of the greatest number.

Adam Smith's grand design of a market economy was adopted extensively in Europe and elsewhere. The march of the commercial and the industrial revolutions enlarged production and trade, and great strides were taken towards generating employment and increasing personal incomes. These were the first major attacks on poverty as real wages rose for those who gained employment. A second benefit received by the working classes was that a larger volume of work became available.

THE GREAT REVOLUTIONS AS MAJOR CAUSES OF POVERTY REDUCTION

The early phases of the industrial revolution appear to have caused an increase in poverty, not only in the colonized areas but also in the home country, as the benefits of improved farming and increased industrial production remained confined to the more resilient elements in society and did not benefit those who were not educated or trained to obtain opportunities in the new lines of production and trade.

Coinciding with the emergence of the market economy, there emerged a series of great revolutions in the late eighteenth, the nineteenth and the twentieth centuries – urbanization, the commercial transformation, and in turn the agricultural, industrial, technological, communications and information revolutions. These cataclysmic occurrences sharpened competition, demolished many a monopoly, hugely enlarged the supply and variety of products to cater to rising demand, cheapened the cost of those products, provided mass availability and made a major dent in poverty.

LIMITATIONS OF THE MARKET ECONOMY AND SHIFT TOWARDS THE WELFARE STATE AND THE PLANNED ECONOMY

However, even after 150 years of the market system, about three-quarters of the world remained poor. Market structures continued to be monopolistic and oligipolistic to a large extent. Moreover, even in the market economies, economic fluctuations persisted and troubled all societies. Poverty continued to prevail extensively, in the Western world during depressions and recessions, and in the under-developed world at all times. These disturbing phenomena, on the one hand, initiated in the developed world the idea and practice of the welfare state and, on the other, led many nations to the notion and practice of the planned economy.

By the end of the nineteenth century, as the phenomenon of mass poverty still persisted in Western Europe and elsewhere, attention came to be focused on human deprivation and distress and a social revolution began to emerge to tackle the problems of poverty in the fields of literacy, education, health, and income and employment. It was no accident that social pressures and trade unionism emerged which demanded legislation for improving employment and earning opportunities for all categories of the labour force. The effect was that the idea of empowerment of deprived groups, including women, emerged and a wide range of socio-economic and political freedoms began to be demanded and provided in order to attack all forms of poverty simultaneously. These great transformations through urbanization, the commercial and industrial revolutions and social reforms made the first impression on mass poverty in Western Europe and created a trend to absorb the poor, in much larger proportions than before, into gainful employment. However, a greater part of the nineteenth and the twentieth centuries was characterized by depressions and recessions which caused considerable fluctuations in poverty, mainly in the industrial world. The twentieth century has, of course, effected a conquest of poverty in the industrialized societies attributable to the increased purchasing power of the poor through a secular increase in employment, mass production of goods and services and greater access to them by the masses at affordable prices. These phenomena have, however, remained confined to the first world only. In the same way the welfare state is essentially a first world anti-poverty organization which has cared for the poor as never before in world history.

But even the welfare state has in due course run into huge budget difficulties which can hurt the poor through the inflation they generate, even if they also provide them with substantial social services. The modern state has not yet found a satisfactory solution to the budget deficits largely caused by social services on the one side and rising government and defence expenditures on the other. Thus, the future of the anti-poverty welfare state hangs in the balance, poised between a desire to continue to provide these great services and a desire to move towards expenditure cuts, balanced budgets and the conquest of inflation. Against this backdrop, various dimensions of poverty are examined in this book. At the outset, some preliminary observations may be made.

ALTERNATIVE DEFINITIONS AND MEASUREMENTS OF POVERTY

While poverty is variously defined in economic and sociological literature, an important aspect of poverty is a subjective feeling of being poor either absolutely or relative to others. As there are insurmountable difficulties arising from both conceptual and statistical limitations, this aspect of subjectivity – a feeling of being poor – is not examined in this study. Even the various objective definitions focusing on the concept of relative deprivation do not lend themselves easily to a measurement of varied forms of poverty. Perhaps none of the measures which are well documented in economic literature is entirely satisfactory. This study too encounters these difficulties, both of definition and of measurement.

Of the various brands and definitions of poverty, the concept of sectoral or segmental poverty is easy to understand and even to estimate. A community or region may be poor in terms of food consumption or calorie intake; in education, health care, shelter and other facilities such as transport and communication. It should be possible, with some degree of arbitrariness, to decide objectively as to what number of calories or volume of foodgrains and other foods and essential amenities is necessary to keep body and soul together on a sustainable basis. This number of calories per capita per day or the volume of average food intake per day can be regarded as a norm and would constitute an absolute measure of poverty, that is to say, a dividing line between the poor and the non-poor. Obviously, the number of people obtaining calories or food or other benefits above such a norm would be deemed to be non-poor and those below the norm would be defined as poor. The percentage of the poor in the total population would then constitute a measure of proportionate poverty. Likewise, segmental poverty in terms of education, health care, etc., can be defined and measured in both absolute and proportionate terms.

Briefly, while there are many dimensions of poverty and many definitions are possible, this study is confined to a set of five different definitions which are:

(i) absolute poverty, that is the absolute number of poor below the defined poverty norm;

(ii) proportionate poverty, that is the proportion of population below the defined norm;

(iii) sectoral poverty defined in absolute and proportionate terms as population below a pre-defined level of literacy, education, health care, etc.;

(iv) a composite index of human development which has recently emerged as a comprehensive index of poverty, determined on the basis of a suitable mix of factors like, income, literacy and life expectancy; and

(v) relative poverty which reflects income distribution.

Applying such data as are available to these alternative measures, various aspects of poverty in different parts of the world are examined. Moreover, in order to establish the direction of change, that is to decide whether poverty is increasing or declining, poverty estimates have been attempted for two points of time in the selected countries. Thus, the analysis lends perspective to various aspects of poverty and endeavours to gauge the degree as well as the direction of deprivation in five major categories of countries.

In all, 24 countries grouped in five different categories are examined in this study. These represent 67 per cent of the world's population and are categorized as follows;

(i) advanced market economies

(ii) planned (socialist) economies

(iii) developing market economies

(iv) mixed economies

(v) least developed economies.

In view of the perceived limitations of various methods and approaches of measuring poverty, this study employs a wide range of indicators grouped under the five alternative definitions mentioned above. These, it is hoped, will enable the reader to reflect on various aspects of poverty in different countries that are at different stages of development.

SOME MACRO-INDICATORS OF POVERTY

An analysis of some macro-level indicators such as gross national product (GNP), gross domestic product (GDP), gross domestic investment and private consumption expenditure reveals the stage of development of an economy as well as the extent to which people reap socio-economic benefits.

There are wide variations in the macro-indicators within and across the five groups of countries.

- It emerges that the developed market economies enjoy a substantially higher GNP and GDP per capita as compared to all other categories.
- However, in these advanced economies, the rate of economic growth has decelerated over time, which spins a tale, perhaps, of secular decline or stagnation.
- In the second category, the planned economies not only experienced low growth rates of 2 per cent or so in the 1980s and 1990s but moved into negative growth rates during recessions. In these command economies of the former Soviet Union and Eastern Europe, it appears that the transition from a planned set-up to a market economy has not come easily, and frictions and maladjustment have dealt a body-blow to growth rates during transition.
- The third category of developing economies has generally done fairly well but within this broad category, the performance of the market-oriented developing economies of East Asia has been perceptibly better than that of the mixed economies. The indicators show that within developing countries, the market-oriented economies have reached a higher level of economic development as compared to the mixed economies. As the direction of change in GNP/GDP per capita is inversely related to poverty, the rapid growth of GDP/GNP per capita in the developing market economies spells a rapid decline in poverty in this category.
- The least developed economies show a mixed trend. The results based on GDP behaviour per capita duly corroborate these findings.

The key variable of gross domestic investment reflects the resources devoted in different countries to accelerating the pace of development. As compared to the previous decade, 1980–90, the rate of gross investment has generally declined in most advanced economies in the 1990s, while some countries have recorded even a negative growth rate. The investment scenario in planned economies is even more grim and has deteriorated at a faster pace. The developing market economies have generally been able to enhance the rate of gross investment but the corresponding rate for most mixed economies has shown a decline. The least developed economies have a very low rate of investment, which indicates a grim prospect for accelerating the pace of economic development.

The extent of improvement in the well-being of people can also be reflected in the rate of change in private consumption expenditure. During the period 1980–93, whereas the advanced market economies have generally recorded a steady improvement in the rate of increase in consumption expenditure, the planned economies showed a dismal result as the improvement was either negligible or negative. Compared to the planned economies, the developing market economies and the mixed economies showed a higher rate of increase of consumption expenditure. The overall consumption situation in the least developed economies remained depressive.

ABSOLUTE AND PROPORTIONATE POVERTY

In almost all the countries, absolute and proportionate poverty has been declining. Some countries are, however, more successful than others in annihilating poverty as the extent of decline in the poverty ratio widely differs across the developing world.

The relevant data pertaining to absolute and proportionate levels of poverty for different countries and regions demonstrate that there is generally a reduction in the number of poor people, the absolute number of whom is very low for the developing market economies but substantial in the mixed economies and the least developed economies.

The poverty ratio, that is the ratio of people in poverty to the total population, is disturbingly high for the mixed and the least developed economies. Whereas the poverty percentage for the developing market economies varies between 5 per cent for Korea and 25 per cent for Indonesia, the corresponding figures for the mixed economies vary between 9 per cent for China and 52 per cent for Kenya. This percentage was 40 for India in the 1990s while for the poorest of the least developed countries, namely Bangladesh and Ethiopia, it was as high as 78 and 60 per cent respectively. It is also clear that poverty is concentrated in the rural areas of most countries. To alleviate the incidence of poverty, almost every country has undertaken some social security measures to protect the poorest of the poor.

The expenditure on social security benefits as a share of GDP indicates that the developed economies spend as much as 16.2 per cent of GDP on social security. The corresponding ratio for the developing countries is very low (China 3.4 per cent and India 0.5 per cent) and greatly varies across the groups and countries.

The index of per capita food production with the base 1979–81 = 100 demonstrates that a few countries have considerably increased the level of production of food per capita while some others have recorded a poor performance. Daily calorie supply per capita is generally higher for the developing market economies – 3298 for Korea and 2884 for Malaysia – as compared to the mixed economies – China 2729 and Pakistan 2316. The corresponding figures for the least developed countries are very low in comparison, with an average of 2100 calories prescribed as a minimum by the World Bank. The figure for India is 2395 calories per capita per day while Brazil and Kenya in the same category of mixed economies have 2824 and 2075 calories per person per day, respectively.

A comparison of two years, i.e. 1970 and 1992, show that the food dependency ratio (the ratio of food imports to food consumption) for most countries has substantially declined. The comparison of countries across the groups shows a mixed trend but it does indicate that in the least developed economies the dependency ratio has increased, especially for Ethiopia and Niger. This ratio has substantially declined in India from 21 per cent in 1970 to 5 per cent in 1992. Among all the countries considered here, India and China are least dependent on the import of food (5 per cent of the total merchandise import). The indices of production of food and calorie supply per capita are, however, higher for China than for India.

Thus, it transpires that the incidence of poverty is falling nearly everywhere but that it is far from being extinguished anywhere. The present poverty reduction is occurring somewhat faster in the developing market economies. The least developed countries are, however, still in the grip of high levels of poverty and require positive intervention through relevant policies and programmes to ensure a decent standard of living for the people.

SECTORAL POVERTY: LITERACY, EDUCATION AND HEALTH

The extent of deprivation in different countries in the areas of social services, mainly literacy, education and health care, were examined in terms of physical attainments and, in some cases, financial allocations.

It is heartening that the first world (Group 1) and the second world (Group 2) countries have almost totally abolished illiteracy, their literacy percentage of adult population ranging between 99 and 95 per cent. This percentage is quite high even in the developing market economies of Group 3 and ranges between 97 and 82 per cent, Saudi Arabia alone having a figure of only 61 per cent. The mixed economies of Group 4 have a range of literacy percentage between 82 (Brazil) and 50 (India). Pakistan alone showing a much lower figure, of 36 per cent. The least developed economies (Group 5) range between 36 per cent (Bangladesh) and 12 per cent (Niger). There is a wide variation in the level of educational efforts, as measured by mean years of schooling across the countries. Whereas this figure is highest for the industrialized countries, averaging 11 to 12 years, the corresponding figure for the least developed countries is the lowest i.e. less than two years. Among the developing countries, the market economies have a higher level of attainment than the mixed economies. Within the developing countries, comparisons show that India's educational effort is one of the lowest, as the mean years of schooling in 1992 was 2.4 years as against 9.3 and 5 years, respectively for Korea and China.

Secondly, the combined enrolment ratio for primary and secondary levels of education, which indicates the extent of educational participation, reveals that the developing countries, particularly the mixed economies and the least developed countries, are lagging far behind the economically better-off countries. This ratio varies from as low as 15 for Niger to as high as 96 for USA. The degree of improvement in this ratio is generally higher for economically better-off countries than for others over the period 1985 to 1993. Thirdly, apart from the quantitative dimensions of educational efforts, the qualitative attributes of education are also more favourable in the relatively advanced countries. For instance, a comparison of student–teacher ratios indicates that this ratio is in favour of developed countries inasmuch as one teacher there handles a small-sized class of as few as 20 students whereas the corresponding size for developing and least developing countries is generally very high – being in the range of 30 to 60 students per class. This obviously affects the quality of education quite adversely.

Fourthly, the availability of science and technology (S&T) personnel per thousand population is much higher in the advanced countries. This indicates the long distance which the developing and least developed countries have yet to travel on the road to industrial and scientific achievements and hence to near self-sufficiency in S&T manpower and an effective management of technology for development.

Fifthly, a higher level of physical attainment in terms of GNP/GDP and investment in the critical sectors of the developed economies is also explained by a higher level of public expenditure on education in relation to the GNP and total public expenditure. Briefly, various indicators of educational efforts, as pointed out above, reveal considerable variations across the countries but demonstrate a positive association between levels of educational attainment and economic development. It is a strong possibility that educational poverty in the developing world is adversely affecting efforts to annihilate various other forms of poverty.

Good health or lack of it is an important component of the quality of life of a people. Efforts made by different countries to provide health-care facilities are reflected in life expectancy at birth. Relevant indicators such as the share of national income spent on health-improving activities, namely provision for hospitals, doctors and nurses, reflect on the extent of effort being made in attacking health poverty.

A higher life expectancy is not the result of health measures alone. Higher per capita income, higher literacy rates and better education and awareness as well as other factors have an impact on life expectancy. Though there are considerable differences in life expectancy across the countries, people in the industrialized countries – developed market economies as well as planned economies – have a relatively longer life span of 70–80 years, as compared to 47–60 years in the developing countries, owing to the availability of better health facilities. Obviously, the advanced countries have succeeded in raising life expectancy above 75 years, and reducing the years of life lost due to premature death. However, there is a perceptible rise in AIDS cases in advanced countries.

Health expenditure as a percentage of GNP is considerably higher in industrialized countries – 6–13 per cent – in comparison with the developing countries – 4 per cent or less. Owing to income constraints poor countries have been spending much less than the amounts required to assure the necessary provisions for health care.

HUMAN DEPRIVATION AND DISTRESS

The phenomenon of human deprivation and distress is found to be widespread in all the countries. While millions of people in economically backward countries are deprived of basic needs such as food, clothing, shelter, clean drinking water, sanitation and other amenities required for decent living, a large number of people in advanced countries are distressed as a result of several problems which are essentially a by-product of industrialization, secular stagnation, recurring recessions and post-development phenomena. These seem to result in unemployment, high crime rates, high divorce rates, drugs, drunkenness and new diseases. In spite of considerable success in augmenting economic opportunities, unemployment rates are observed to be very high both in the developed market economies and the formerly planned economies. The range is as high as 7–15 per cent in 1993. However, for some countries like Japan and the Russian Federation, unemployment was as low as 2.5 and 0.8 per cent, respectively, though the latter figure conceals a good deal of under-employment. Socio-economic crime rates are also inordinately high despite significant improvements in income, health facilities and levels of education. The relevant data reveal that the number of prisoners, homicides, drug related crimes, adult rapes and suicides is very high, thereby indicating a high level of human distress.

LEVELS OF HUMAN DEVELOPMENT

The human development index (HDI) is widely accepted as a composite index of the quality of life which incorporates, within itself, such vital factors as GNP per capita, life expectancy at birth and educational attainment of the people. The HDI indicates the distance that various countries have yet to travel on the road to poverty annihilation. Though the HDI, as a measure of poverty, is not free from blemishes, it is useful when assessing the performance of various countries, on a comparable basis, in improving the socio-economic conditions of the people. The results show that while HDI is generally very high for the developed economies, it has deteriorated over the period 1985 to 1993. Such a deterioration is particularly noticeable in the planned economies and clearly indicates a fall in the quality of life in the former socialist countries as compared to the levels attained in the past. The developing and the least developed economies register a clear improvement in the HDI between 1985 and 1993, but the index is too low for most countries, thus indicating the serious nature of poverty of all forms.

International Differences in Poverty Levels

An assessment of international differences in poverty levels, measured in terms of a broad index of purchasing power parity (PPP) estimate of GNP per capita, reveal glaring differences across the countries. As compared to the US GNP per capita which is taken as 100 for the years 1987 and 1994, the index shows that between these years

(i) most of the advanced countries realized an increase in their per capita income levels;

(ii) the planned economies recorded a substantial deterioration in their per capita income;

(iii) the developing market economies improved their per capita income considerably; whereas

(iv) the developing mixed economies and least developed countries showed a mixed trend.

Another dimension of relative poverty is revealed from the examination of the pattern of distribution of income and consumption among different groups of the countries. The results demonstrate that there is a narrower range of disparity in the planned economies as compared to the advanced market economies. This reflects a particular concern in the erstwhile planned economies for a somewhat equitable distribution of income and expenditure. This is also corroborated by the Gini Index. Per capita income disparity in other groups of countries shows a mixed trend – wide disparity in Brazil and Kenya and relatively narrow in Bangladesh, Pakistan and Indonesia. In general, quite understandably, there is concentration of poverty in the lower income brackets.

SOME REFLECTIONS ON THE NATURE OF POVERTY

1. Poverty Increases during the Initial Phases of Growth

The process of economic growth in the initial stages of development is generally accompanied by a maldistribution of income and wealth. The beneficiaries of the growth process are generally the active agents in the process who receive benefits while the economically less resilient members of the society, who constitute a significant majority, get left behind. This causes an adverse distribution of income and wealth for those who are already poor and no country that has developed its economy seems to be an exception to this experience. Generally too, the process of economic growth is accompanied by inflation and there seem to be very few societies which have moved from stagnation to economic growth without inflation. As the main engine of growth is investment, it appears that the demand-generating effects of investment normally run ahead of the supply-generating effects of the same investment and this slackness of supplies relative to demand results in price increases, almost invariably. Now, as the process of inflation itself is maldistributive in nature and favours manufacturers, surplus-producing farmers, traders and debtors as against workers, consumers and creditors, the maldistribution of income and wealth, inherent in the initial growth process, is sharpened through inflation itself. Maldistribution adversely affects the economically weaker sections of society; and as it emerges from two major sources – the growth process and the inflationary process – its obvious outcome is poverty enhancement.

Poverty thus tends to increase in early phases of the growth process until, at a later stage, the benefits of development, in terms of enhanced real wages and other real incomes, begin to reach the bulk of people. But the issue of the uplift of the poor from poverty is clinched only when the benefits of mass-produced consumer goods – produced with scale economies and improved technologies – become available to the masses of population, alongside the rise in real wages.

2. Growth Does Not Trickle Down Easily into the Poverty Zones

Another characteristic of the growth process is that economic growth does not trickle down easily to the masses, especially in low-growth economies. It is only in the high-growth economies, such as those of the ASEAN region, (before the debacle of 1998) that a high per capita growth rate seems to percolate among the lower rungs of the population and involves them in economic activity, often through the market forces. But such a percolation or trickle-down does not occur in low-growth economies which, therefore, operate major programmes of economic development in the hope of uplifting the poor. Countries like India which had a zero or even a negative per capita growth of real incomes in the first half of the twentieth century and a mere 1 per cent per capita growth during four decades of the second half (1951–91) had to launch several employment – and income – generating schemes as a substitute for the trickle-down of economic growth. In the last fifteen years or so there has been considerable improvement in the growth of per capita income – currently increasing by more than 5 per cent in many countries due to a reduction in the population growth rate, on the one side, and an increase in income growth and people's participation in economic activity on the other. This has resulted in a reduction in the poverty ratio – as in India from 48 per cent in the early 1950s to 31–39 per cent in the early 1990s. The situation augurs well for poverty reduction in the coming years as poverty-stricken people are becoming more involved in the growth process and the indicators of progress have begun to exhibit the same tendency.

3. Price and Quantity Controls Do Not Augment Supplies

In fact, economic growth trickles down into the poverty zones more through the augmentation of supplies with the market forces rather than through the management of demand, as practised in the controlled and semi-controlled economies. As controlled prices and quantities depress supplies and prolong the controls, these create and multiply the shortages. There is thus a strong tendency on the part of the population, especially in the higher income groups, to offer a price higher than the controlled price built into the public distribution system. The producers and sellers wish to sell only at the free-market prices which, being illegal, cannot be declared and are called black market prices. Controlled prices thus create a market situation in which huge 'black' earnings are generated from illegal sales at illegal prices. The black incomes thus earned become an enemy of equitable income distribution as they escape the tax net; they are also enemies of economic growth as they cannot be declared and used in institutional investment, say, through the stock exchanges. In such a maldistributed set-up, anti-poverty mechanisms become the major casualty and prosperity is confined to the traditionally elite society. In such regimes, populations living in the poverty zones never get the benefit of abundantly supplied goods and services at affordable prices, nor the benefits of scale economies and new technologies. Living as they do on the brink of survival, with only a thin cushion against destitution, economic crises become the characteristic features of command and semi-command economies which then become the hub of poverty.

In the poorer areas of the world, failure of the command economy to eliminate poverty has led to the creation of the alternative system of liberalization, de-control, de-licensing and deregulation and a return to the market economy with an enlargement of the areas of free market operation. The relevant set of measures, almost opposite to those in the hitherto prevailing set-up, goes under the name of structural adjustment programme and has been in vogue intensively since the end of the decade of 1980s.

4. Structural Adjustment Programmes

Governments of many developing countries have adopted structural adjustment programmes in different degrees as a means, among other things, of eliminating poverty. These programmes generally consist of a cut in governmental and public sector activity, privatization of infrastructures, production, trade and transport, reduction of subsidies and tax rates, reduction in budget deficits and fiscal deficits, market determination of foreign exchange rate of the local currency and a shift towards export generation in place of import substitution. Some scepticism has been expressed on the grounds of normative and positive considerations about the effectiveness of structural reform in reducing poverty; but economic logic suggests that removal of the licensing system to remove oligopolies and the admission of a larger number of producers would increase the volume of production, intensify competition among producers and reduce prices. As goods and services of mass consumption become available at low and affordable prices, the stage is set for the reduction and elimination of poverty in countries which have undertaken structural reform. The market economy has, however, its negative aspects as well in that monopolies and oligopolies are also a part of the market economy and are replete with negative results in terms of growth and poverty annihilation.

POVERTY IN HIGHLY DEVELOPED MARKET ECONOMIES

The effect of the great revolutions, namely urbanization, agricultural transformation and commercial, industrial and technological break-throughs, which occurred in the nineteenth and twentieth centuries, was virtually to conquer the problem of poverty in North America, Western Europe, Australia and Japan. The progress of rationality, the shift from autocratic to democratic regimes, the emergence of trade unionism and women's freedom, the evolution of the welfare state, and so on created a dynamism in economic, social and political organizations as well as a network of social services which promoted economic growth and social development. The industrialized economies with market orientation continued to progress, which enabled them not only to annihilate poverty but also to overcome the impact of two long-lasting and bloody wars of the first half of the twentieth century. However, the market economies were subjected to violent economic fluctuations due to the phenomenon of the trade cycle. Fluctuations in the growth of income, investment and employment had the effect of cyclical fluctuations in poverty levels. During the periodic occurrence of recessions and depressions the poorer population in the industrialized states suffered even though these states had evolved social safety nets to protect the poor. However, as the revenues of these governments also decline during recessions, the social services are subjected to great strain and this causes a fear of reduction, if they are not actually reduced. The occurrence of recessions is the basic cause of unemployment and allied phenomena which, in turn, lead to a resurgence of poverty. A characteristic feature of recessions is a declining rate of return on capital stock. Even as newer technology tends to enhance the rate of return to capital, the consequent abundance of capital stock in highly competitive situations causes a decline in the rate of return and slows down the rate of increase of capital. Also, a large availability of capital stock, resulting in a large availability of consumer goods works towards a saturation of demand or results in a decline in incremental demand at the margin. Consequently, profitability of capital and consumer goods declines and that suppresses the rate of investment and reduces income generation. This is duly borne out by the evidence on the rate of growth of GNP/GDP for different industrialized countries. The lower rate of return to capital and the declining demand at the margin seem to be strong factors behind a decline in investment rates, which, in turn, aggravate unemployment, particularly during recessionary periods. This is true for almost all the industrialized countries.

The declining growth rates of GNP, the languishing and sluggish rates of investment and the exorbitant and perhaps growing rates of unemployment in the Western economies suggest that the conquest of poverty achieved earlier in the twentieth century is turning into defeat. Newer dimensions of poverty and perhaps newer forms have been emerging in these industrialized market economies. The high levels of economic performance, the large capital stock and state-of-the-art technologies may serve to cover up the fact of emerging poverty, confined as it is to pockets of unemployment. What also obscures poverty is the capability built up in these economies to provide comprehensive social services and unemployment benefits which cushion the impact of emerging poverty – and this is what matters crucially.

Perhaps the immediate as well as the long-term solutions to the problem of recurring recessions are to be found in:

- nuclear and non-nuclear disarmament, and turning the resources saved into 'peace dividends' for gains in the civilian economy;
- augmentation of trade with other areas of the world in Asia, Latin America and Africa; and
- generation of employment in the production and foreign trade sectors.

This last approach by the advanced countries to save themselves from poverty and the necessary conditions required to implement this method are matters which require the resolution of many a thorny issue but also have a vast potential for the conquest of the remaining poverty in the industrialized and fast-developing economies.

SOME FEATURES OF POVERTY DYNAMICS

It is by now received wisdom that 'Poverty anywhere is a danger to prosperity everywhere.' Hence, the concern of the world to alleviate poverty. The methodology of poverty measurement in vogue at present has been debatable owing to many conceptual and statistical problems; and therefore the norms of income or expenditure or calorie values do not reflect the degree of change in poverty. In the use of calorie norms, as a measure of poverty, a major problem arises from the fact that people are bound rather rigidly by traditional food habits and do not change these very much even when they become prosperous. Indices of poverty based on calories or food consumption thus have a built-in depressor within themselves and fail to note the improvements in the non-food realm of poverty.

People appear to try to get out of non-food poverty, mainly the poverty of education, health, shelter and industrial consumer goods, rather faster than they annihilate food poverty itself. Also, personal expenditure data do not capture the massive consumption of subsidized goods and services provided by the state. Personal expenditure data thus grossly understate the annihilation or reduction of poverty through public goods. It is important, therefore, to study the phenomenon of poverty by considering food as well as non-food items of expenditure and examine the degree of achievement in order to gain an idea about the extent of reduction in different forms of poverty.

Poverty elimination is a slow process especially in countries with a history of colonial domination and laissez-faire governments. When colonial domination ends and popular governments responsive to public opinion emerge, then, if all goes well with the process of planned development, the elimination of poverty generally proceeds through three phases. To illustrate with the help of just one brand of poverty – that is literacy poverty:

1. The characteristics of the first phase are: national income declines or rises very slowly, population keeps on rising, per capita income declines, the percentage of literates may rise but the absolute number of illiterates increases.
2. In phase two, with national independence, some basic changes occur as the state makes a concerted effort to devote resources for economic development. The national income rises, though slowly, high growth in population is checked, the percentage of literate, educated and healthy population increases and the percentage of the illiterate, uneducated and unhealthy people decreases.
3. In phase three, some structural changes emerge. The process of mass production begins, per capita income rises, percentage of literate, educated and healthy people rises faster and not only the percentage but the absolute number of poor and illiterate persons begins to decline faster.

Poverty in India

Using the example of India, an assessment of various forms and phases of poverty reveals some interesting dynamics.

1. The poverty ratio has declined from 51.5 per cent in 1951 to 37 per cent in 1991. The corresponding number of poor has, however, increased from 186 m to 350 m, which undoubtedly indicates the chronic nature of poverty.
2. The poverty of literacy has diminished over the period 1951 to 1991 as the increase in the number of literates (298 m) is higher than the

increase in number of illiterates (131 m). Thus, the literacy percentage has risen from 18 to 52 per cent whereas illiteracy has declined from 82 to 48 per cent. However, the absolute number of illiterates – a staggering 377 m in 1991 compared to 359 m literates in 1957 – has been seriously dampening the improvement.

3. The phenomenon of poverty also exhibits itself in lack of education. But there has been a substantial reduction in educational poverty during the planning era, beginning from 1951. Enrolment ratio for high/higher secondary education has recorded a six-fold increase, i.e. from 5 per cent in 1951 to 29.5 per cent in 1993. Likewise, for post-secondary education, the ratio has recorded a 12-fold increase. The proportion of matriculates and graduates to the total population has, accordingly, increased six and seven times, respectively. These evidences indicate considerable increase in the stock of educated and trained manpower or reduction in educational poverty.

4. As regards poverty of health, it is difficult to evolve a yardstick to measure health conditions. However, indicators of access to health facilities, information on death rates, life expectancy at birth, and so on, provide an idea of the extent of reduction in health poverty. The results show substantial improvement in life expectancy from 32 years in 1951 to 61 years in 1993 which is attributable to improved facilities for health care. This is borne out by increased coverage of the population served by (a) hospital beds, from 31 per cent in 1951 to 76 per cent in 1991, (b) primary health centres in rural areas from 21 per cent in 1961 to 97 per cent in 1995, and (c) rural health centres from 14 per cent in 1961 to 82 per cent in 1993. Thus, by all accounts, health poverty is sharply on the decline.

Finally, an overall assessment demonstrates that improvement in per capita income, above 1 per cent per annum, was too low to uplift the poor which is to say that economic growth was not trickling down. Now, since the observed rate of improvement in per capita income, above 3 per cent per annum in the last decade, is much higher than in the first three decades of planning, we might expect the poor to be lifted up faster in the foreseeable future especially as a result of increased levels of government expenditure on 'public goods and services' such as education, health, shelter, drinking water, sanitation, and the like. If the delivery of India's massive poverty alleviation programmes improves, reduction in poverty could be expedited even faster. The upshot clearly is that the old notion of a chronic persistence of poverty both in absolute and percentage terms has to be given up and alternative methodologies of poverty estimation, such as the

Human Development Index, focusing on the total quality of life rather than calorie or food consumption, and including the consumption of public goods rather than personal expenditures alone, have to be evolved.

STRATEGIES FOR POVERTY REDUCTION IN DIFFERENT REGIMES

Nearly all politico-economic regimes in different periods have had the issues of economic growth, income redistribution and poverty reduction built into their economic philosophies, either explicitly or implicitly. These, however, did not have a specifically defined strategy for poverty reduction. Poverty reduction was seen as an implicit end-product which will finally emerge as a result of the interactions of demand and supply, the release of market forces, the urge to expand through competition, keeping prices low, profits normal and technology improving all the time, the final result being the greatest good of the greatest number. This market strategy did not rule out the existence and the emergence of unemployment from time to time especially during the down-swing and the recessionary phases of the trade cycle. But it was asserted that in such situations competition among the workers would lead to a decline in wages and lower wage rates would then enhance employment once again, until full employment is reached – and poverty reduction would be a function of full employment. The many 'ifs' and 'buts' in reaching the stage of full employment and poverty reduction were of course noted and debated but it was hoped that eventually this stage would be reached.

In the market economies, great strides were taken towards the promotion of phenomenal economic growth which involved the working classes in rising employment and eventually gave them periodic full employment, enlarging social services such as health, education and unemployment benefits, and at a later stage made the working classes the recipients of mass-produced and affordable consumer goods and services. The developing market economies – designated collectively as the first world – benefited from the coexistence of the phenomena of urbanization, commercialization, industrialization and agricultural transformation in the nineteenth and the early twentieth centuries and the advantage of technological revolutions in the later twentieth century. In other words, the economic philosophy of the market place coexisted with these great socio-economic revolutions and substantially impacted poverty. Nevertheless, poverty could not be totally conquered and the biblical statement of seven lean years followed by seven fat years, with some modifications of the numbers, remained a fact of economic life.

What lessons can be gained from the past regimes for a future onslaught on the remaining poverty in these regions? One is that the continuation and the strengthening of the market economy and the forces of liberalization is an essential policy ingredient and should be continued – albeit with some major qualifications and additional policies. The second conclusion from historical experience is that the market economy is a necessary but not a sufficient mechanism if total elimination of poverty is the objective. In other words, the market economy has to be tempered by some other prescriptions inasmuch as the existence and the recurrence of the trade cycle with its depressions and recoveries, its down-turns and up-turns, detracts from the trend towards growth of the market economies and causes poverty to recur again and again, making millions of people move from prosperity to poverty. The recurring cycle thus makes poverty persist and does not guarantee either full employment or a continued improvement in public welfare. Anti-cyclical policies, a shift from balanced budgets to periodic deficit spending, the launching of public works programmes and the installation of safety nets in the shape of social service programmes, all turn out to be necessary adjuncts to the continuation of the market economy.

The welfare state (which was a mechanism seemingly opposite to the market economy but actually an adjunct of it) has evolved in the twentieth century, particularly in the market economies. The welfare state had its roots in Western Europe only in the post-World War II period but was clearly practised as an answer to the negative aspects of the market economy. Nevertheless, the welfare state did not invalidate the market economy but modified it here and there and provided for interventions in all the major West European economies. It sometimes went under the name of democratic socialism or social democracy and, whatever its name, sought to provide cushions for the working and middle classes against the evils of depressions and inflation. This phase in the market economies did result in a redistribution of income in favour of the middle and working classes and modified some of the extreme situations prevailing earlier – of towering heights of prosperity on the one side and disturbing depths of depression on the other.

In the planned economies and the communist states, a succession of Five Year Plans of economic development, the elimination of private property, the organization of farm workers into collective and state farms and the prohibition of private profits, rents, foreign trade and employment of one man by another, were some of the key characteristics of economic organization. With all their strictness, the hang-over of a bloody revolution and autocratic decision making by an economic oligarchy, the planned economies can, nevertheless, be credited with huge capital formation, increase in output, increase in employment, improved income and wealth distribution, better housing, education and health measures and a substantial reduction in poverty. However, the lack of freedom of enterprise, an absence of the incentive to private property and the exploitation inherent in an autocratic economic system, detracted greatly from public welfare and from the quality of the economic system, not to mention the miseries caused by a dictatorial and unaccountable political regime which was responsible for many an injustice and considerable inequity.

In these planned regimes, the system today is in a state of flux, trying to return from the command economy to the market economy and, meanwhile, by all accounts, poverty has come out into the open and seems to be on the increase.

THE MIXED ECONOMY APPROACH TO POVERTY REDUCTION

Dissatisfied with the performance of the market economies on the one side and the centrally planned economies on the other, a large number of developing countries in Asia, Latin America and Africa, seized with the problem of growth, development and poverty reduction, adopted the mixed economy model. This consisted largely of allowing the markets to function in some sectors and sub-sectors while practising market interventions in other sectors in different ways and in varying degrees.

The institution of a Planning Commission in many cases, the operation of government-sponsored industries in the public sector, the construction of basic infrastructures such as electric power, road transportation, production of steel and non-ferrous metals, mining ventures, irrigation projects and fertilizer plants to strengthen the agricultural sector and to produce abundant food and raw material were common features of the planning strategies. Investment was encouraged, both in the public and the private sectors, in these mixed economies but the construction of basic infrastructures in projects which had large forward and backward linkages was designed to work in the public sector of enterprise. Measures for literacy, education and health improvement also remained generally the responsibility of the government though private organizations were allowed to work in these areas.

In many of these economies, as a result of various programmes of development, poverty was reduced either overall or in particular sectors and segments. The process of continuing investment in all the major sectors, the march of industrialization, the rise in agricultural productivity – thanks to the green revolution in several countries – greater opportunities for employment and greater attention to educational and health measures, did cause an improvement in economic levels and raised the standard of living of the poor in most developing countries. In some countries, though not in all, the control of inflation also helped the poor and the rich alike.

Exasperated by the slow progress of economic development and poverty reduction and facing a series of economic crises, in the late 1980s and the first half of the 1990s a large number of developing countries have launched a process of structural reforms. These reforms have many dimensions but they invariably include a reduction of price, investment, foreign-exchange, import and export controls and many other restrictions, in particular, the industrial licensing, rationing and quota systems. The reforms also include a cut in the budget deficits and fiscal deficit as a proportion of the GDP, a reduction in tax rates, both direct and indirect, a correction of the over-value of local currencies through devaluation and freer flow of foreign capital into the domestic economies. These reforms have worked with different degrees of success in the last few years but the process is still incomplete inasmuch as the reforms have remained confined to a few functional areas and sectors and still leave the liberalization and deregulation of many sectors to the future.

Though the reforms do not always speak explicitly of poverty reduction, it is clear that there is a major strategy for poverty reduction implicit in the structural reform process. This consists of the elimination of a monopoly of one firm and an oligopoly of a few firms by providing entry without licences to many competitive firms in each sector and allowing the competition to take its own course. This is expected to put pressure on the inefficient firms and either lead to their closure or a merger or amalgamation with other more efficient firms or a takeover of the inefficient ones by the efficient. The surviving firms will have greater efficiency and lower costs per unit of output through enlarged levels of production and economies of scale, access to new technologies and better management. The fact that they will be working in a competitive and non-oligopolistic environment will guarantee their efficiency and profitability and, in due course, lead to the emergence of mass-produced goods and services. As the scales of production widen, employment will increase too and larger incomes will be the necessary outcome. With larger incomes and greater purchasing power through employment and higher profitability on the demand side and with large-scale supplies of mass-produced goods, the poor would begin to have access in large numbers to efficient goods and services and would be raised from poverty in due course.

A PACKAGE OF POLICIES FOR POVERTY ELIMINATION

It is now possible to prescribe a package of policies and practices for eliminating the huge volume of poverty that still remains in all categories of nations.

The market economy is a basic condition for stimulating growth, expanding employment and poverty reduction. Observation of the economic and social phenomena in the eighteenth and nineteenth centuries makes it clear that the expansion of the market economy in Western Europe and North America coexisted with the unfolding of the great socio-economic revolutions – urban, commercial, agricultural and industrial. It is debatable whether the market economy drove the great revolutions or whether the revolutions gave an impetus to the market economy. However, the coexistence of the two ground-breaking occurrences is undeniable and it is also very probable that the two phenomena were mutually reinforcing.

The combined effects of these revolutions, aided and abetted by the market economy, and vice versa, have certainly transformed the West European and the North American scene and brought about a surge of affluence on the one hand and a decline in poverty on the other. This is another compelling reason why the present and the future efforts to reduce or eliminate poverty should not fail to move in the direction of introducing and strengthening market forces, as this is one of the prime ways to cause the great economic revolutions in regimes in which these have not yet arrived or are arriving hesitantly. Poverty reduction is a certainty when the commercial, agricultural and industrial revolutions occur and the strengthening of the market economy does seem to be a significant cause of these occurrences. Thus, the first recommendation for poverty reduction is to launch all possible efforts to establish or re-establish the market economy where it has been superseded by other systems and to strengthen it where it is weak. It is necessary in the context of a well-performing market economy to evolve legislation and practices for the elimination of the weaknesses of the market economy such as monopoly and oligopoly, allow freedom of entry into various lines of production, set up professional and expert institutions for promoting and monitoring public and private enterprises, preventing deviations and malpractices and protecting consumer interest.

What has to be picked up from the socialist experiment for a universal effort for poverty reduction is the will of the state – to which has to be added the will of the society – to launch programmes of sustainable literacy, education, health, housing and employment. Some of the details of the techniques to put the will of the state into practice can also be borrowed from the Soviet and East European experiment, but others have to be shunned and avoided, in particular the colossal intervention and interference of political dictatorship and rigid bureaucracy. Accountable institutions and professional bodies – rather than governments and officialdom – should manage these great objectives and programmes for poverty elimination. In like manner, if any part of the future strategy of poverty reduction in democratic countries is to be borrowed from the welfare state, it is the provision of sustainable social services for such matters as literacy, education, health, medicine, housing, employment and various arrangements for unemployment compensation, social insurance, old age pensions and maternity benefits.

These measures of structural reform, which have replaced the tenets of the semi-planned mixed economies such as price and quantity controls, licensing systems and government-owned enterprise with liberalizing measures, are still unfolding in the developing nations. In these developing, semi-planned and mixed economies, the introduction of a great deal of respect for the forces of demand and supply is essential. Policy makers must recognize that over-regulation does not pay, that monopolies and oligopolies in production and trade have to be replaced, through free entry of new firms, by a competitive economy; that the private sector of enterprise as well as the NGO sector has to be given greater freedom to invest, expand and perform; that the public sector should also be subjected to structural reform and be given the same freedoms as the private sector; that in the event of non-performance even after the new freedoms, the public enterprise should become the subject of what is called disinvestment and, perhaps, handed over to private enterprise; that import of technologies from abroad as well as desirable consumer goods should be allowed more freely; and that in order to get these technologies, a freer flow of foreign capital has to be allowed, perhaps with some consideration for disallowing, in the early stages of reform, the acquisition of local enterprises by foreign firms, in order to prevent takeovers and amalgamations by external parties – at any rate, for an initial period.

THE RE-EMERGENCE OF POVERTY OWING TO RECESSION IN THE ASIAN ECONOMIES

The steady trend in economic growth and poverty eradication was arrested suddenly by a startling collapse in many fundamentals of the East Asian economies, which were gripped by an almost unforeseen recession in 1997 and 1998. Currency values, GDP per capita, industrial production, exports and imports as well as the expectations of steady growth collapsed with astonishing rapidity. The banking system revealed serious chinks in its armour and went into a tailspin as regards the mobilization of resources, loans to corporate business and the financing of industrial and commercial ventures. The market economy, which was the latest showpiece among the exhibits of the Eastern economies of Korea, Thailand, Malaysia, Indonesia, the Philippines and, indeed, the highly developed economy of Japan, suddenly revealed that it was not infallible. The impact of the collapse was, of course, felt most intensively within the South Asian countries. But the fall-out effects of this collapse travelled far and wide, even, to a smaller degree in the United States, Australia and the European economies of the first world.

The causes of the Eastern recession are a matter of detailed analysis and have many dimensions and contributory factors; but whatever the causes, it has been fully established that industrial production, trade and commerce, banking services, the stock markets, the real estate market, the house building industry, and both the export trade and imports, all moved downward suddenly, sharply impacting the GDP and the domestic demand on the one side, and domestic supplies and external trade on the other. As usually happens in a recession, the former buoyant expectations of commodity markets, land markets and stock markets were suddenly replaced by depressing sentiments.

While the robust economy of the US had come out of recession in 1996 and beyond, the West European economies were continuing to show very sluggish growth in 1996 and 1997. These continuing recessionary tendencies, in a large part of the first world, were already depressing the exports of East Asia and South Asia substantially and noticeably. In this deflationary context, the sudden emergence of a recession in the East Asian economies compounded the decline. The depressed production in East Asia, together with the sudden decline of the banking systems, reduced East Asian exports and moderately impacted the GDP and other basic factors in the first world, while the negative impact was quite serious in South Asia. The recessionary factors seemed finally to bring about a serious downturn in employment, and via unemployment a reduction in the purchasing power of the people and a resurgence of poverty. The same decline in employment, incomes and purchasing power caused a cut-back in the provisions for health and education, especially in the educational and health-oriented social services.

Economic analysts noted in 1998 that Japan, the most achievement-oriented country in the East, was about to be caught up 'in a vicious cycle', where a drop in demand for products causes a fall in prices, which in turn causes profits to be squeezed, adversely affecting wages and jobs; this then brings about even lower demand. It seemed that the world's second largest economy was about to enter its worst deflationary period for many years. Arguing that 'the global effects of the crisis would very likely be "more severe" than initially forecast', the IMF 'revised its world economic growth forecast for 1998 to 3.1%, down from its forecast of 4.3% six months ago'. An IMF report also forecast that 'the three economies most affected by the Asian crisis would diminish this year: Indonesia would contract by 5%, Thailand by 3.1% and Korea by 0.8%'. For Japan, the IMF forecast zero growth in 1998 while its chief economist warned that even zero growth 'may not materialize' this year. For China too which 'has been relatively immune to contagion from the crisis', the IMF forecast a slow-down to about 7 per cent growth in 1998 compared with 8.8 per cent in 1997. The IMF also said that

> spill-over from the Asian crisis was most apparent in Russia, Ukraine and Estonia. Russia's economy will grow just 1% in 1998 while African growth forecast was lowered to 4.6% from 5% and that for the Middle East to 3.3% from 4.2%.

The dollar values of domestic currencies in South Asia declined sharply, some through devaluation and others through a depreciation in the foreign exchange market.

The impact in South Asia was relatively constrained. The Indian rupee declined from Rs 39 to the dollar to Rs 42.5 between 1997 and 1998 while the Indian growth rate of GDP declined from 7 per cent to 5 per cent between 1996 and 1998. The unemployment rate in all the Eastern countries surged, rising in Japan to a record 3.6 per cent as the number of unemployed reached 2.46 million from 160,000 a year earlier – the highest unemployment rate since Tokyo started compiling data in 1953. In China, despite the relative immunity of the Chinese economy from East Asian as well as world influences, and despite the non-convertibility of China's currency on world markets, 'the hazards of accumulating bad loans and the potential for financial collapse have begun to register in Beijing' .... The upshot over time has been a thorough undermining of the nation's banking system and analysts are inclined to argue that 'the Chinese banking system is currently insolvent'.

While an investigation of the causality of the recession and the measurement of its depth is still being undertaken, the net outcome in the East Asian economies, including Japan and China, and in the South Asian economies, including India, is an augmentation of unemployment, a decline in incomes and purchasing power and, in the context of weak or non-existent social services (barring Japan), an absolute decline in public welfare. Millions of non-poor in the region have moved into the zone of poverty. Serious efforts are in progress in all these countries to overcome the recession through increases in government expenditure, construction of infrastructures and other public works and the launching of fiscal measures such as lower tax rates; but the re-emergence of the economies from recession and their return to the track of employment enhancement and poverty eradication still seems a far cry.

It is clear that poverty will finally be reduced when the following things happen:

1. With efficient production of goods and services and abundant supplies thereafter – and with the adoption of appropriate fiscal and monetary policies – the inflation rates slow down.
2. When the non-competitive and inefficient firms collapse or merge with the efficient ones, surpluses are generated *en masse* and larger employment and entitlements of well-trained and efficient labour takes place against this surplus generation – thus causing profits and wage incomes among the masses of the people to rise.
3. When mass-produced consumer goods and durable consumer goods can be accessed by the poor with higher employment and higher incomes and at affordable prices.
4. When the governments begin to acquire surpluses to launch social services to cushion the poor.
5. When the renewed and recurring cycles of recession are conquered through a much better macro-management of the world economies.

Part I
The Nature of Poverty

1 Introduction

Towards the close of the twentieth century, poverty and deprivation still appear to be universal phenomena discernible everywhere in the world. It is possible to hypothesize, with some degree of credibility, that while most countries and regions of the world are experiencing an increase in affluence to a greater or lesser extent, in virtually no country or region of the world can the existence of poverty be denied. In fact, in many parts of the globe, poverty seems to be on the rise, engulfing an increasing number of people or reducing the position of the poor in relation to the rich. In the last quarter-century, while national and international fora have discussed the possibility of a world economic order, the prevailing scenario is still of world economic disorder.

The subject of this disorder relates to five major categories of nations in the world today:

(i) the industrialized and developed nations of the first world in North America, Western Europe, Japan, Australia and New Zealand;
(ii) the planned economies of the second world i.e. Russia, the other ex-Soviet States and the Eastern European States;
(iii) the developing, high-growth market economies of the Far East such as Korea and Indonesia;
(iv) the developing mixed economies of Asia, Africa and Latin America, consisting of such countries as Brazil, China and India; and
(v) the low-income and least developed countries of the third world many of which have not yet quite broken away from stagnation, such as Niger and Ethiopia.

Each of these five categories of nations is experiencing either a persistence of poverty or the emergence of new poverty in the midst of growing prosperity. This hypothesis, however strong, needs to be tested and established so that appropriate solutions for balanced economic growth and poverty elimination can be proposed to suit the different situations and circumstances. This book seeks to analyse world trends in economic growth through studying representative nations in the aforementioned categories, but focuses particularly on the areas of widespread stagnation, existing and emerging poverty, economic disorder and industrial recession.

In the course of research for this book, we selected and analysed four or five representative countries in each of the five categories of nations, estimated poverty in various ways, reflected on the reasons for the persistence of poverty and the causes of newly emerging poverty, and sought some solutions using market forces or other means.

1. Among the advanced industrial economies of the first world, the approach is to conduct an analysis of poverty and economic growth in the USA, Western Europe, Japan and Australia. Particular attention will be paid to recurring recessions, the slow-down in economic growth, increasing unemployment, rising budget deficits, the adverse balance of payments and the emergence of new poverty. The research work seeks to obtain an answer to the basic question whether there is a secular stagnation in industrialized societies leading to new forms of poverty. Causalities will be discussed and solutions sought.

2. In respect of the countries of the second world, the former Soviet Union and the countries of East Europe the analysis takes note of the end of the socialist era and the attempt to switch over to private sector operations and the market economy. But it focuses on the current inability of the ex-socialist regimes to give birth to privatized industry, agriculture and trade and to operate the market economy so as to increase employment and reduce poverty. The inflationary phenomenon and the sharp decline in the foreign exchange rates of some currencies, with the Russian rouble declining to several hundred roubles, compared to one rouble to a dollar only a few years ago, and the impact of this on new poverty is also noted. The research asks how these economies of the second world can smooth their transition from a command economy to a market economy and from public ownership of property to private ownership; and reflects on the volumes of investment from other parts of the world, as well as domestic investment, required to set these economies on the path of economic growth and to annihilate the current and increasing problem of poverty.

3. Within the third world, the project distinguishes the case of the so-called Asian Tigers – Korea, Taiwan and the ASEAN countries which have not only broken away from stagnation but have established a high rate of economic and industrial growth, large capital formation and a functioning of the market economy. There will be reflections on the lessons for rapid growth and poverty annihilation that can be learnt in these countries, especially after the recent recession.

4. Most Latin American, African and Asian countries, including Brazil, China, India and Nigeria, have also broken away from stagnation and are well on the way to economic growth. Nevertheless, huge areas of poverty still persist and in some of these economies there is currently

a failure to reduce unemployment and enhance industrial and agricultural growth. The book explores whether new moves towards structural adjustments, in other words a switch from semi-command economies to market economies and the strategy of privatization and reduced reliance on public enterprise, are adequate to put these 'non-tigerized' developing countries on the track of economic stability, high employment, improved social safety nets and poverty reduction.

5. There are then the remaining countries of the fifth category, often termed 'least developed countries' (LDCs) which have not really broken away from stagnation and are the scene of persistent poverty and deprivation of a disturbing nature. These countries have not yet set themselves squarely on the path of industrial, agricultural and overall economic growth. The book considers what strategies would be relevant for breaking away from stagnation and what role the private and the public sector institutions, on the one hand, and the market economy and state support, on the other, could play in achieving the objectives of growth with poverty reduction, and equity without inefficiency.

Among other instruments of research and analysis, in Part II the book focuses on various indices of poverty, such as the macro-indices of GNP and GDP per capita, percentage poverty (i.e. percentage of population below a defined poverty line) and sectoral poverty, as well as a measure of the quality of life in terms of the human development index (HDI). It then applies these indices to representative countries in each of the five categories of nations in order to determine the degree of poverty on various criteria.

After reflecting on the reasons for the persistence of poverty or the causes of emerging poverty in Part III the book seeks different solutions in different contexts, especially through the instrumentation of liberalization, deregulation and the market economy and, where necessary, through state intervention. It examines the role of the state through its operation in and assistance to the social sectors of education and health, the role of private enterprise as the major mechanism for development and poverty eradication through the mass production of efficient and affordable consumer goods and services, as well as the role of NGOs as one of the most potent mechanisms for poverty removal.

Particular attention is devoted in this work to the Indian situation with regard to poverty behaviour. The sponsors of the research, the Economic and Scientific Foundation, desired a focused treatment of India, and working in India, we have a substantial volume of data and information which could be utilized with profit. Hence, there is a specific chapter on poverty in India and on the various attempts to deal with it.

In our research we have attempted to estimate five different measures of poverty, at two points of time, in 24 representative countries of the world, classified into five different categories of nations in the so-called first, second and third worlds. Towards the end of the book (Chapter 15), we endeavour to cull, from the four or five different economic systems prevailing in the world in the last 150 years or so, the approaches and attempts to reduce or eliminate poverty and examine their success and failures. And finally, in Chapter 16, there is an attempt to learn from the failures of different economic systems and put together a package of basic recommendations – not detailed policies – which in today's circum- stances, at the threshold of the twenty-first century, could still lead to the removal of a significant volume of the remaining poverty.

2 Persistence of Poverty and Early Attempts to Eradicate it

IMBALANCE BETWEEN POPULATION AND RESOURCES

In pre-industrial societies, many areas of the world where population was in approximate balance with natural resources tended to avoid the problem of mass poverty. High death rates, owing to a near absence of health measures, kept the growth rate of population in check and in an approximate balance with the availability of easily exploitable natural resources such as land, water and mineral stocks. The 'wisdom of the ages' did cater for the provision of indigenous health practices and a slight increase in population and labour force, while small improvements in agricultural practices, handicrafts and services led to some increase in output. Thus, a balance could be maintained between population and resources in many societies. This population-resources balance continued for many centuries in several regions and mass poverty did not arise. Even so, the distribution of income in such societies never tended towards equality. A feudal organization of society and hierarchical social structures spelled inequality and economic and social differentiation among groups of people, and this phenomenon was a drag on further growth and development.

However, the absence of technological breakthroughs in the pre-industrial era, together with over-exploitation of natural resources did disturb the population-resources balance in many regions and either kept those regions at a low level of existence or worsened the poverty situation. Owing to over-exploitation of land, the incidence of, for example, soil depletion, erosion, deforestation and the drying up of sources of water and mineral wealth caused major reductions in employment, self-employment and incomes and hence poverty became widespread and proliferated to a substantial degree.

In such deteriorating situations some populations attempted to migrate to new settlements in areas where more resources were available. But those settlements and areas also came to be subjected, in due course, to similar occurrences, similar imbalances and a similar emergence of poverty. Thus, in the pre-industrial revolution era, poverty became a generalized phenomenon and coexisted with prosperity in small or large measure.

35

THE VICIOUS CIRCLE OF POVERTY

In pre-industrial as in post-industrial times, there seems to have been yet another built-in phenomenon which tended to perpetuate poverty. This has been analysed competently by Ragnar Nurkse (1953) under the caption of 'vicious circle of poverty'. Societies with low productivity per person naturally tend to have low per capita incomes and hence become the scene of low savings and low investment in relation to incomes. A small rate of saving obviously goes with small investment or capital formation and, as the productivity depends primarily on the volume of capital with which labour works, productivity per person tends to remain low, and this becomes the cause, once again, of low per capita income.

The vicious circle is completed as low per capita incomes in turn generate low savings, low investment and small productivity per person. Many societies for decades and centuries continue to be subjected to this vicious circle of poverty and the day never comes when a breakthrough might occur and higher economic growth might arise. This phenomenon, among other things, explains the persistence and even the proliferation of poverty. There are many other economic, social and political causes of poverty which can be observed in various societies and this is how poverty remains a persistent feature of numerous areas of the world.

COLONIZATION

The impact of colonial denomination, mostly by European powers, on Asia, Africa and Latin America, seems to have caused two opposite effects on poverty in these continents. On the one hand is the story of exploitation – the organization of the colonial economies with the primary purpose of benefiting the colonial powers; the exodus of cheaply purchased or freely taken raw materials such as cotton, jute and mineral wealth or treasures; the production of goods back home at low cost with the use of cheap raw materials, and the sale of these goods in the colonized areas at high prices; the imposition of high taxation in the colonies, together with the suppression of the local urges of the colonial people – which spells a massive expansion of poverty and a suppression of economic growth and local capabilities. On the other hand, there were some contributions made by the colonial powers in colonial areas (mostly for their own benefit) such as the development of railways and ports, the laying of country-wide roads, the construction of hill stations and the establishment of some factories and plantations of tea, coffee and other products – some for military and governmental purpose and others to accommodate industry from the home country in the colonized areas. The latter contributions may have caused the generation of some employment, some education, some local expertise and the training of some personnel, both in the colonies and back home. But, in general, it was the former phenomenon of domination and exploitation that led to massive exploitation and expansion of poverty in these areas.

HOW ECONOMIC GROWTH EMERGES AND POVERTY IS REDUCED

What, then, causes a break from poverty and initiates the phenomenon of economic growth or rapid growth is the subject of various economic theories, and in these theories, often rooted in real experience, many causes of growth have been identified. These are mostly unpredictable and often accidental. For one thing, there could be a major discovery of mineral wealth or of major sources of water. For another, there could emerge some means to exploit this wealth through technological innovations. Yet another cause could be the migration of resilient sections of populations from areas of economic saturation and decline to greener pastures where these migrated groups apply their resilience and initiate a take off into economic growth, in turn providing larger opportunities and poverty reduction.

Yet another factor, which has been known to convert stagnation into growth, is the emergence of dynamic leadership which guides societies towards saving, investment, work and higher productivity. The prime example of this phenomenon of growth generated through leadership is the emergence of Protestant ethics in Western Europe. The impact of leaders like Calvin and Martin Luther and the evolution of Protestant ethics which led people to save more, invest more, economize on frivolous consumption and work harder, has been known to be a revolutionary occurrence which generated a new zeal and enthusiasm for economic betterment as well as social development.

This new ideology even caused the migration of people from the frustrating environment of traditional and rigidly organized societies to areas of better opportunity where the new ideology could be practised with conspicuous success. The migrations of many groups from Western Europe to North America, where a free environment and abundant resources were available for exploitation, has been a significant cause of the economic uplift of these groups and the rapid development of those very areas of free and rich environment. Similarly, in the Arabian and Middle Eastern societies of the early Middle Ages, the leadership of the Prophet Mohammed with his emphasis on 'halal' (legitimate) consumption and avoidance of 'haram' (illegitimate) consumption, on austerity and 'bait-ul-mal' (public welfare fund), his exhortation to legitimate pursuits such as trade and 'hijrat' (migration), and the colossal emphasis on learning and knowledge, led to a revolutionary situation, in which Greek learning and Indian mathematics were absorbed by the rapidly expanding Islamic world, while at the same time deductive disciplines such as algebra, calculus, astronomy and philosophy were discovered, and experimental disciplines such as chemistry, medicine, geography and ship-building, were invented and propagated. These developments brought about a unification of the scientific method by combining deduction and induction, theory and experimentation: all of these, taken together, gave Islamic scientific work an unbelievable resilience, and brought about a breakthrough in various Muslim societies and economies – extended over several hundred years, as economic and social development occurred – as a result of which poverty seems to have been confined to relatively small areas during that period.

In India, the teachings of Mahatma Gandhi, which emphasized austerity, simplicity, saving and investment, handicraft and small industry, and the liberation of down-trodden castes, seems to have generated an astonishing desire for freedom and liberty which within a half-century caused the end of colonial domination and prepared the ground for economic growth and social development. Of course, it took a long time for these phenomena to impact on the poverty situation and reduce the colossal impoverishment and deprivation of Indian society. But finally the phenomenon of economic growth is taking over and major dents in poverty now seem to be in evidence.

THE GREAT ECONOMIC REVOLUTIONS AS A CAUSE OF POVERTY REDUCTION

Towards the end of the eighteenth and the beginning of the nineteenth centuries, a series of great economic revolutions began to sweep Western Europe and, in due course, began to have some impact on economic growth and development in other areas of the world as well. The earlier impact of the Renaissance and of the Protestant Reformation began to show itself in many different ways in the late eighteenth and the nineteenth centuries. The gathering of small village populations in both small and large urban concentrations in towns and cities, led to an internal dialogue on economic and social matters in these new, larger units of population.

The phenomenon of urbanization had a far-reaching impact. The cluster of large populations in towns and cities necessitated trade between these units, unlike the relatively self-reliant situation obtaining in small villages. This became the cause of a commercial revolution which, in turn, promoted the ideas of competitiveness, the organization of supplies which catered to rising demands and the determination of market prices to equate demand and supply and generate normal profits. For the purpose of cost reduction and saleability of goods and services in these competitive population centres, further ideas of technological development and innovations emerged – and the sum total of these phenomena could be termed a commercial revolution.

Simultaneously, to feed the new urban societies in an environment of supply responding to demand, the agricultural product had to be expanded and ways of enhancing agricultural productivity were destined to emerge. This agricultural transformation occurred in many European societies in the nineteenth century. On the other side of the Atlantic two major developments were taking place, also of a revolutionary nature where, with new freedoms and a competitive environment, a major industrial and agricultural revolution was taking place which was destined in the twentieth century to make the United States a leading world power in economic as well as political terms and prepared the background, through mass production, for the absorption of the poor in fruitful occupations and counter-poverty engagements.

The simultaneous march of urbanization and commercialization prepared the ground for the great industrial revolution with its numerous innovations and inventions in factory production, corporate organization and transport development on land and sea. Simultaneously, the free market economy was becoming strong and this brought to an end many over-regulations and interventions by the state and many elements of the guild system which, in numerous cases, were a drag on enhanced production.

Primarily, in this environment, it was the discovery of the steam engine and its application to numerous ventures on sea and land, including the steamship, the railways and factory production, that changed the scene and gave new hope for poverty reduction. Then came the discovery of electric power, the shift from steam locomotives to the electrification of the railways and, in the twentieth century, the invention of the automobile, as well as numerous other breakthroughs in technology which stamped the industrial revolution on the face of Europe and North America and even began to spread many aspects of that revolution into colonial areas as well. The phenomenal expansion of demand for various goods and services by income earners employed in all these expanded and innovative ventures, and the organization of supplies to meet this demand with ever-improving technologies led to massive increases in production and, with automation, economies of scale and cost reduction, launched the era of mass production of goods and services.

The early phases of the industrial revolution are a story of increased poverty, not only in the colonized countries but also in the home countries as the benefits of improved farming, enhanced trade and transportation and increased industrial production remained confined to the more resilient elements in society and did not spread to those who were not educated or trained to take advantage of opportunities in the new lines of production and trade. By the end of the nineteenth century, the phenomenon of mass poverty, which still persisted in Western Europe and North America, began to attract attention and a social revolution began to emerge to tackle the problem of literacy, education, health, employment and income poverty. It was no accident that Acts of European parliaments and legislative assemblies began to focus on literacy, primary and secondary education and health measures and sanitation. It was also no coincidence that just at this time trade unionism emerged, a movement which demanded legislation and social organization to lift up the unemployed into employment and transfer those already employed into better employment with economic and social benefits. The liberties of women also came to be stressed by social groups which forced the state to legislate for family freedoms and liberties and to give women voting rights and other benefits. This last movement, in later years, became the progenitor of the idea of empowerment of women. It was again in the end of the nineteenth and the beginning of the twentieth century that the limited franchise in national and local government elections was extended beyond the land-based and property-based franchise to universal suffrage, first for the adult male population and, in due course, the female population. In sum, these great transformations through the urban revolution, the commercial revolution, the industrial revolution and social reforms began to make deep indentures in Western Europe and the United States into mass poverty and began to absorb the poor in much larger proportions than before in gainful employment.

POVERTY SURVIVES AND INCREASES DURING DEPRESSIONS AND RECESSIONS

However, the nineteenth and twentieth centuries remained – despite a trend towards poverty reduction – eras of highly disturbing economic fluctuations, exhibited in the trade cycles, with an average duration of six to seven years – good years followed by lean years and recoveries followed by depressions. Poverty fluctuated vastly during these ups and downs – declining during recoveries and increasing during depressions and recessions. The Great Depression (1929–33) seems to have spread all over the world with its epicentre in the United States and another in Western Europe, but not omitting colonized areas or other parts of the globe. Poverty became the ruling phenomenon during these depressions; and even when the depressions were over, periodic recessions, which exhibited fluctuations of a slightly smaller dimension, remained the order of the day in industrialized societies.

But depressions and recessions apart, it is true that the twentieth century has seen the conquest of poverty in the industrialized societies as a secular trend. The clue to this conquest seems to lie in the mass production of goods and services which cheapens their price in relation to incomes, and makes these accessible to the poorer segments of the population, lifting them up to a decent level of consumption on the one hand and greater levels of employment on the other, thus enabling them to buy those goods and services. However, until recently this reduction of poverty through increased employment and mass availability of goods and services could not be said to be the ruling phenomenon outside the first world – that is, outside Western Europe, the United States, Canada, Australia, New Zealand and a few other pockets.

The failure within the first world to eliminate poverty totally – due to economic fluctuations and their allied effects – led to great social concern and produced the phenomenon of the welfare state. Here, employment and social benefits became the focal points and various states began to organize social services and employment benefits to cushion the poor of working age who were in permanent or temporary unemployment for one reason or another or were the victims of periodic joblessness. Unemployment benefits were the main concern of the welfare state but no less important was the provision of old age pensions, maternity benefits, educational benefits and massive health services which took care of the poor as never before in world history. The provision of these cushions seems to have become a durable and perhaps an irreversible feature of industrial societies – so much so that governments can fall on whether they are supportive of these services or wish to dilute them for one reason or other.

The welfare state has certainly been an anti-poverty organization but it has run into dozens of difficulties. Its most disturbing trouble has been the high and expanding costs of social services and unemployment benefits which often go beyond the capability of the state to raise the necessary resources through taxation and other ways. The consequent budget deficits were generally inflationary in nature and hurt the poor even if they had the benefit of social services. The modern state has not yet found a sustainable solution to this problem, which is largely caused by social services on the one side and rising defence expenditure on the other. Thus, the future of the anti-poor welfare state hangs in the balance, poised between the will to continue to provide these great services on one hand and, on the other, a desire to move on towards a budget balance and the conquest of inflation. Meanwhile, other forms of politico-economic organizations emerged outside the welfare state – the planned economy in the second world and the so-called mixed economy in various parts of the third world.

3 Advent of the Market Economy and its Impact on Poverty

During the second half of the eighteenth and the whole of the nineteenth and the twentieth centuries, about half a dozen epoch-making economic systems were evolved with the express intent of uplifting masses of people economically and reducing or eliminating poverty. Prominent among these in the eighteenth and the nineteenth centuries was the free market economy which coexisted with the great revolutionary movements mentioned in Chapter 2. These revolutionary movements could not have been sustained under the interventionist and market-unfriendly organizational set-up of the eighteenth and early nineteenth centuries. It would be equally true to say that the restrictive and interventionist structures of those times could not stand the strains and stresses of the revolutionary changes and had to be blown away. As the 'powers of production', that is to say the power which society has over the utilization of resources, altered dramatically, a different economic ideology was required to support and sustain the newly emerging structures of production, domestic and foreign trade, and transportation. With the changing powers of production, the 'relations of production', that is the relations in which the consumers, producers, traders and the workforce are linked together, had to alter – and this is what happened alongside those great economic revolutions.

The pundit of the new idea of the market economy was Adam Smith who, in his seminal work *An Enquiry into the Nature and Causes of the Wealth of Nations*, formulated a new structure of thought which brushed aside the interventionist, semi-controlled and restrictive regimes of the pre-industrial revolutionary era and laid down the principles of competitiveness, free trade and freely organized market economy. This new theoretical structure, when put into practice, was expected to pull out societies from the depths of poverty and bring about the 'greatest good of the greatest number'.

On the eve of the agricultural and the industrial revolutions, the economies of Western Europe and, for that matter, of many other parts of the world, were either feudal or interventionist in nature and did not respect the forces of demand and supply. In Western Europe in particular, monopolies and oligopolies were the order of the day. The medieval guilds, among other features, prevented the entry of new producers and traders into the production system. The guilds were organized to admit and train new entrants in specific lines of goods and services and to limit the number of entrants strictly so that supplies would not increase too much and prices and wages would not decline and collapse.

In addition, the state itself followed restrictive policies and was not accustomed to the idea of freedom in production, trade and commerce. In the agricultural sector, the system of bonded labour still prevailed extensively in many places, and the farm workers, tied to the farms where they were born, were not allowed to seek employment and higher wages elsewhere. They could be punished severely if they so much as talked of mobility, let alone acted upon it. Their wages were extremely low and presumably did not rise *pari passu* with a rise in the price of the product they produced. In other words, the economies of the eighteenth and the early nineteenth centuries were riddled with interventions, controls and lack of mobility and the producing and trading agents were not in a position to operate freely.

Though there were other earlier formulators of some propositions of free trade, free markets and competitiveness, Adam Smith was the genius who codified, so to speak, the various prescriptions and brought them together into a master-treatise of the market economy, and knit them into a self-contained and logical economic system. Adam Smith's formulations swept aside the numerous cobwebs of restrictions, licences and controls and established a new doctrine which spread not only across Western Europe but also in the United States and by stages in various other parts of the world. Smith's propositions of the free market economy could be said in many respects to be the nineteenth-century counterparts of the late-twentieth-century ideas of liberalization, deregulation and globalization which are today floating around in the developing economies of Asia, Latin America and Africa.

Adam Smith argued for a free economy where competition would prevail among the producers, traders and workers – both within their own categories and across different categories. He brushed aside the concepts of controls, restrictions, interventions and bonded labour. For centuries the encashment of labour had been prevalent in England, so that a family of agricultural workers could make a payment to the landlord by which they purchased their freedom to move out to seek employment in other farms or in industry. Smith supported mobility which, he argued, was an essential part of competitiveness. In his theory, consumers were the key decision makers about what goods and services to demand and in what quantities and at what prices to demand them. Consumers' sovereignty was to be the

watch-word and, depending upon their tastes, their incomes and the prevailing prices, the consumers would demand certain quantities of goods
and services. The producers, like so many minions serving the consumers,
would respond to the demand and produce whatever was demanded. To be
able to produce that, they would call forth the necessary labour and raw
material at certain prices and wages. The workers, like so many respon-
dents to the wage rates and the volume of employment offered, would provide their services to the producers. As consumers demanded more, prices
would rise and as suppliers supplied more goods, prices would fall. The
equilibrium price is one at which demand and supply are in balance and
the market is cleared. Similarly, in the markets for raw material and
labour, the demand for these items by producers meets a response from the
suppliers of raw material and labour in certain volumes and at certain
prices and wages. The markets for these items are also cleared at a price at
which demand and supply of material and labour are in equilibrium.

Basically, Smith's formulations substituted, for decisions by the state,
guilds and other agencies, decisions by individual and corporate units, with
freedom of operation, competitiveness and mobility. In other words,
instead of this or that authority deciding such matters as supply, demand
and prices, the 'invisible hand of nature' would determine these factors
without the intervention of any visible agency. Smith further argued that in
a competitive economy profits would tend to be reasonable. Should an
outburst of demand raise the price of a good or service, a corresponding
outburst of supplies would bring prices to normal and profits also to a normal level. Moreover, the desire for higher profits would lead producers to
innovate, inventing new methods and new technologies of production. The
innovator or the inventor would, no doubt, reap high profits immediately
after a successful innovation or invention was accepted by the market; but
soon the proliferation of this invention, among other users, and counter-
inventions by other inventors, would bring down the profits of the earlier
inventor or innovator. Thus, in the market economy, the consumer's sovereignty would prevail, while producers and workers would respond to
consumer demand, prices would be determined by demand and supply,
innovations and inventions would be continuous, and profits, though high
at times, would tend to a competitive normalcy. The invisible 'hand of
nature' would guide the system without a dictator, an autocrat, a bureau-
crat or a monopolist determining the economic fortunes of society.

Adam Smith's grand design of the market economy spread like wildfire
and over the years was adopted extensively. The interventionist control
systems were demolished, mobility was promoted, free trade (at any rate
in Western Europe) came to be practised widely and the benefits of the

market economy, in terms of innovations, economies of large-scale production and various forms of efficiency, were widely visible. Smith's theorizing was the ideological counterpart, so to speak, of the agricultural, commercial and industrial revolutions and had far-reaching acceptability and impact wherever in the world these revolutions travelled. To the extent that the market economies, together with the march of the commercial and industrial revolutions, enlarged production, domestic trade and foreign trade, the labour force expanded enormously. On the whole, there was a massive spread and growth of employment and the first major dents in poverty were registered. To the extent that real wages also rose among those who obtained employment, a second benefit was received by the working classes in addition to a larger volume of work and employment.

While the impact of the free market economy was deep as well as widespread and led to a huge improvement in the standard of living of many peoples in many parts of the world, it must be stated that after 150 years of the operation of the market system, a large part of the world remained a poor place. Even in the market economies, economic fluctuations pestered all societies. The biblical statement of seven fat years followed by seven lean years seemed to repeat itself with slightly modified time spans and the trade cycle or business cycle began to impact the market economies negatively.

Outside Western Europe, North America, Australia, New Zealand and Japan, a large number of under-developed (or developing) economies were becoming the scene of market orientation in many sectors. Nevertheless, these pockets of liberalization could not proliferate in the rest of the economy and the shortage of capital stock, paucity of employment and large prevalence of under-employment or concealed unemployment remained a negative feature. Meanwhile, in the industrialized or developed world, poverty continued to be extensively in evidence, especially during depressions and recessions, and in the developing world it continued to prevail all the time. The failure to conquer poverty and the disturbing phenomena associated with it led to two quite opposite developments: in the (developed) first world, it generated the idea and practice of the welfare state, and, in the second world, it promoted the notion and practice of the Communist revolution and the planned economy. Third world (under-developed) countries in the second half of the twentieth century generally adopted the pattern of a mixed economy combining a sort of economic planning using the market mechanism with a good deal of intervention and quantitative control. But none of these efforts really eradicated the persistent problem of poverty and substantial structural reforms had to be invoked in the hope of establishing sustainable economic growth and minimizing poverty.

Part II
Measurements of Poverty

4 Alternative Definitions and Measurements of Poverty

Terrible poverty appears to be a universal phenomenon and it is possible to hypothesize, with some degree of credibility, that while most countries and regions of the world are experiencing an improvement in affluence to a smaller or greater extent, in virtually no country or region can the existence of poverty be denied. In fact, in many parts of the world – both countries and regions – poverty seems to be on the rise, engulfing an increasing number of people or reducing the position of the poor in relation to the rich. This hypothesis about a simultaneous existence of poverty and affluence in all parts of the globe, including the industrialized and highly developed nations, and an increase in poverty in many parts, in absolute, proportionate, relative or indexed terms, has to be tested and either established or rejected – wholly or partly.

VARIOUS DEFINITIONS OF POVERTY

Moreover, even as the meaning of absolute, proportionate and relative poverty and other concepts such as sectoral or segmented poverty would have to be established by means of rigorous definitions, the very term 'poverty' needs a working definition. An important aspect of poverty is a subjective feeling of being poor either absolutely or relative to others, but such a subjective definition, as distinct from objective definitions, is difficult to handle. The difficulty in dealing with subjectivity – a *feeling* of being poor – can be understood by a classic definition of poverty attributable to Socrates: Contentment is natural wealth and greed is forced poverty. Since such emotions as contentment and greed are very subjective, this definition of poverty will not be pursued in this work.

However, economists and social scientists have evolved a concept of deprivation which can be taken into account alongside the various objective definitions. While the definitions of poverty are many and varied, the measurement of these varied forms is even more difficult. On close examination it can be seen that when it comes to measurement, perhaps none of the measures is entirely satisfactory and free from blemish. We will face these difficulties, both of definition and of measurement, as this work proceeds.

Among the various brands and definitions of poverty, perhaps the easiest to understand, and even to estimate, is sectoral or segmental poverty. A community, a nation or a region, may be poor in terms of food consumption or calorie consumption; it may also be poor in literacy and education, or in health and medical facilities, or in housing, or transportation and so on. It should be possible, no doubt, with some degree of arbitrariness, to decide objectively what number of calories or what volume of grain or other foods is necessary to keep body and soul together on a sustainable basis. This average number of calories per capita per day or this volume of average food intake per day, per month or per year, can be regarded as a norm and would constitute an absolute measure of poverty. The number of people obtaining calories or food or other benefits above this norm would be deemed to be non-poor and those below the norm can be defined as poor. The population below the norm of calorie or food poverty in proportion to the total population will constitute a measure of proportionate poverty. In that case, say, 30 or 40 or 50 per cent of the people can be deemed to be poor in food and calorie terms.

In like manner, it should be possible to estimate the absolute number of people in a country or region or a community who are literate, as also the number that are illiterate. Now, the definition of literacy or illiteracy itself poses a problem. Should we define as literate those who know the alphabet and can sign their name, or those who can read or write sentences, or those who can read fluently without hesitation with an extensive vocabulary? Thus, there can be weak as well as strong definitions of literacy and it is possible that different societies have different norms in this respect. Moreover, it is observed that people who are marginally literate (with a weak definition of literacy) can fall back into illiteracy with the lapse of time. In that case, some would be classified as illiterate though they had been literate earlier. Perhaps this problem can be overcome by taking note of literacy poverty only at the time of estimation. Once literacy poverty is defined for a given country or region, the absolute numbers qualifying and not qualifying on this definition will be deemed to be literate or illiterate and the proportion of illiterates to total population could be a measure of literacy poverty. At least one further qualification, however, is that young people, say below the age of 5, 6 or 7, cannot become literate owing to their natural physiology. These children of a very young age are neither literate nor illiterate but illiterable at that age, as the question of illiteracy cannot apply to them. In a suitable numerical description of literates or illiterates, these have to be excluded and the percentage of illiterates so redefined would be deemed to be the percentage of illiterates above the age of 5, 6 or 7, in relation to the total population.

Similarly, one can define educational poverty in absolute or proportionate terms and set up a minimum qualification such as a high school certificate or a degree certificate. However, not everybody in a society ends up with graduation at the bachelor's degree level nor even at the high school (matriculation) level, say at age 16, 17 or 18. But, it is conceivable that even on criteria other than matriculation, a diploma or a degree certificate, a person can be regarded as educated. In a discussion on the ability of an illiterate population to vote sensibly and meaningfully, with a reasonable understanding of issues and personalities involved in a national election, some participants asserted that literacy as such is not an important criterion for exercising voting rights as, in many countries of the world, 'there are millions of educated people who have never been literate!' The reference to 'educated people' here is to the innate wisdom of people, or whole populations, who have passed through thick and thin and have become worldly wise or informed of basic value systems – which qualifies them to be called 'educated'.

MEASURING CHANGES IN POVERTY IN FIVE DIFFERENT WAYS

As there are many dimensions of poverty and many definitions are possible, this study aims at examining various parts of the world on at least five different definitions of poverty:

(i)   absolute poverty, that is the absolute number of poor;
(ii) proportionate poverty, that is the overall percentage of population below a suitably defined poverty line – such as calorie consumption at given levels in different parts of the world;
(iii) sectoral poverty, again defined in absolute and proportionate terms as population above or below a pre-defined level of (a) literacy, (b) education, (c) health etc.;
(iv) the poverty or wealth status level of different societies according to a human development index which attempts to sum up the levels of a population in terms of income, education and life expectancy (the latter itself being the resultant of several factors); and
(v)   relative poverty which reflects income distribution among different deciles of a population, summed up in such terms as a Lorenz Curve or Gini Coefficient.

The estimates, as far as possible, of these alternative measures of poverty are sought from available data for two different points of time a few years apart. This two-points-of-time estimation is undertaken to bring out changes in poverty over time. Is poverty increasing or decreasing within a nation, a region or a category of the world's population on each of the criteria described earlier? Is a decline in poverty over time, or an increase therein, a universal phenomenon in all major categories of the world's population or is it confined to some countries, some regions or some categories of population? Even if poverty is not growing in all countries/categories, is it growing in absolute terms, in other words in terms of the number of people involved in all these countries/categories?

Studying World Poverty in 24 Countries in Five Categories

This two-points-of-time study of five alternative dimensions of poverty which informs this research is being undertaken in five different categories of countries. These are:

(i)   the advanced market economies;
(ii) the planned (socialist) economies;
(iii) the developing market economies;
(iv) the mixed economies with market forces and quantitative controls working simultaneously; and
(v)   the least developed countries.

These will be referred to in this book in abbreviated titles, as (1) advanced economies, (2) planned economies, (3) developing market economies, (4) developing mixed economies, and (5) least developed economies (LDCs). Typical examples of these five varieties respectively are the USA, the USSR/Russia, Korea, India and Ethiopia.

In each of these five categories spread all over the world, we select five countries, except that in category 5 of the least developed economies, only four countries have been selected both for reasons of paucity of data and the small number of such countries available for examination. Essentially it is a purposive selection of countries in each category such that the major countries are not omitted and the countries which are known to be typical of that category as also those which lie at the extreme economic levels of each category are not neglected. This selection, based on a wide spread and typicality as well as inclusion of extreme cases within each category, results in the following 24 countries being selected, which together accounted for 67 per cent of the total world population in 1992 (Table 4.1). Thus, we study poverty under different definitions and apply different ways of measurement as none of the definitions or methods of estimation turns out to be entirely satisfactory. Some definitions seem to be more comprehensive than others but none describes the phenomenon of poverty fully.

Table 4.1
**Identification of Selected Countries in Different Groups based on
Economic Characteristics and Levels of Development**

Country	Region	Population (Million) 1992	Real GDP per capita (PPP$) 1992	Rank
(1)	(2)	(3)	(4)	(5)
1. Developed market economies				
USA	North America	255.2	23 760	1
Japan	East Asia	124.2	20 520	8
Australia	South Pacific	17.4	18 220	18
UK	European Union	57.8	17 160	23
2. Planned economies				
Hungary	East Europe	10.3	6 580	50
Poland	East Europe	38.3	4 830	71
Ukraine	CIS	51.6	5 010	68
Kazakhstan	CIS	16.9	4 270	74
Ukraine	CIS	51.6	5 010	68
3. Developing market economies				
Korea	East Asia	43.7	9 250	38
Singapore	East Asia	2.8	18 330	16
Malaysia	S.E. Asia	18.8	7 790	45
Indonesia	S.E. Asia	188.7	2 950	99
Saudi Arabia	Arab	16.8	9 880	33
4. Mixed economies				
Brazil	Latin America	153.8	5 240	64
China	East Asia	1183.6	1 950	123
Pakistan	South Asia	129.3	2 890	100
India	South Asia	884.4	1 230	141
Kenya	Africa	25.4	1 400	137
5. Least developed economies				
Bangladesh	South Asia	112.7	1 230	141
Cambodia	S.E. Asia	9.4	1 250	140
Ethiopia	East Africa	50.3	330	174
Niger	Africa	8.3	820	156

Notes:
1. The countries are grouped according to major characteristics.
2. The selection of countries in each sub-group is purposive and they broadly represent different regions, levels of development and economic systems.

Source: Compiled from *Human Development Report*, 1995, UNDP.

Indices of poverty which claim our attention first are obviously per capita income and per capita consumption. These descriptions of poverty do not go very far. These are average figures which can, of course, differentiate one population from another so that if the average for one country is higher than the average for another by say, 20 per cent, a presumption can emerge that the country with a higher average is better off in general, relative to the country with a lower average. However, while these average figures can be and are used for ranking or differentiating between different countries, these suffer from all the limitations from which an average figure suffers. Such an average says nothing about the extreme values above or below the average, that is to say, the spread or the range on both sides of the average; nor does it describe the intensity of the poverty (or whatever is being measured) experienced by different groups or deciles of the population above and below the average. For example, country 'A' can have the richest population at an extreme 1000 per cent above the poorest and 100 per cent below the average while country 'B' with the same average can have the richest at a level 100 per cent above the poorest and 50 per cent below the average. Comparisons are thus substantially vitiated and the spread as well as the intensity of poverty in successive groups of population is missed out completely if only average figures such as per capita income and consumption are used.

The other disadvantage of an average estimation such as per capita income of a country or a region is that this per capita figure may be well above or well below the poverty line (the level of per capita income that can be deemed to be separating the rich from the poor). For example, if the average per capita income of a country is $2000 per annum and the poverty line in that country can be defined, after detailed examination, to be $1000 per annum, then the average per capita income is far above and, therefore, does not reflect the poverty line. A separate poverty line in terms of per capita income or consumption has thus to be worked out, rendering the average per capita income or consumption that much removed from a satisfactory estimation of the poverty line. In this very important sense, the population above and below the average per capita income or consumption cannot be described as non-poor or poor respectively.

Thus, while it is useful to work with per capita income and consumption for certain limited purposes, we have to move on to other forms and measures of poverty in order to get closer to a better definition, description and estimation of poverty. This brings us to the next definition of poverty, that is to say, proportionate poverty.

A level of income, consumption or calorie consumption is often determined, in different geographical and cultural contexts, so as to yield a minimum sustainable figure which will

(a) keep body and soul together, or
(b) over and above this, allow a certain level of comfort or amenities for the family, or
(c) additionally provide some minimum level of education and health etc.

There is a minimum physical content of such definitions but there is also a cultural content which is obviously different from place to place and, indeed, from one period to another. In India, for example, a prevailing norm for defining poverty is a calorie value of 2100 for the rural and 2400 for the urban population. In income terms, in 1983, the figure that was used to define the poverty line was a per family income of Rs6108 per annum for rural and Rs7050 per annum for urban families. With the passage of time and with changes in inflation rates as well as secular changes, this figure was raised to Rs12,624 (rural) and Rs14,568 (urban) while the calorie norms remained the same. As we move from one country to another, the same differentiation in the levels of calorie or per capita income/consumption are in evidence; and there too the figures keep changing from time to time with inflationary, secular and other factors. Often these figures are not just the result of guesswork but are painstakingly arrived at through family income or expenditure or food consumption surveys many of which are highly meritorious in their conception and estimates. In India's case, for example, the National Sample Survey (NSS), a survey of considerable technical merit, is the generator of the income, consumption and calorie levels per capita or per family mentioned above.

These surveys result in dividing the population of a country into a number of income or expenditure brackets and estimating the income or expenditure levels of a sample population in each bracket or decile. Once the poverty line – in terms of per capita income, expenditure or calorie consumption, for example – is determined, the people below the poverty line are regarded as poor and those above the poverty line as non-poor. These would be absolute figures such as 20 million poor and 30 million non-poor; and the changes over time in these absolute numbers are also meaningful in that they reflect whether poverty in absolute terms is increasing or decreasing – and if so at what pace.

These absolute numbers of people below and above the poverty line can also be converted into a proportion of total population and this proportion yields the proportionate share of the poor in the total. If the total population is 50 million and the people below the poverty line are 20 million, then 40 per cent of the population would be deemed to be poor and 60 per cent non-poor. These estimates of the absolute number of poor and non-poor, the changes in these absolute numbers between the first and the second point of time and the percentage of people below and above the poverty line, as well as changes in these proportions over time, have been, as far as possible, estimated in this research for all the 24 countries and the five categories.

Estimations of the absolute number as well as the proportion of the poor are not perfect. For one thing, as the poverty line keeps on altering with secular changes or other factors – and has generally to be lowered with progress – the estimations made in the interim period between one change of the poverty line and another may be erroneous. That is to say, if the number of poor, and hence their percentage of total population, is increasing or decreasing steadily, and the poverty line is changed, say, once in ten years, the estimated number and percentage of the poor during the interim will not be fully reliable as, theoretically speaking, the poverty line itself should have been altered smoothly and regularly every year.

Another problem is that as poverty lines in different countries are different, depending upon geographic, economic, demographic, social and cultural factors, and as these poverty lines are raised or lowered at different intervals in different countries, international comparisons of absolute numbers and percentages of the population of the poor cannot be made in any meaningful way. It is for such reasons that while attempting to estimate absolute and percentage poverty in the manner described above, one has to add on the other measures of poverty which may minimize the aforementioned errors – though it is conceivable and even probable that the alternative estimates would be subject to other hazards.

Two or three other weaknesses of poverty estimations based on per capita income or calorie consumption can be noted. An inherent limitation of calorie-based poverty estimates or per capita income-based estimates – when these per capita incomes are themselves tied to a level which satisfies a given calorie value – is that as people's level of living in terms of consumption of goods and services improves, their calorie consumption does not improve in the same proportion. This point needs to be explained in some detail. When very poor people, whose calorie consumption per day is substantially sub-normal, improve their calorie intake, their general level of living, perhaps, moves up *pari passu* with their calorie uplift, as calories are the most crucial item in their consumption. But after a point, human stomach capacity being limited, people do not go on increasing their food intake or cereal intake or calorie intake proportionately with other improvements in their levels of living. When an adult person has reached a calorie consumption of, say, 2200 per day his calorie intake will increase only marginally with other improvements; that is to say, the other improvements will run ahead and faster than food consumption or calorie intake. The point is brought into full relief when we consider that the income elasticity of demand for food, after a certain level of income, may be 0.5. But the income elasticity of demand for radio sets, TV sets, bicycles, scooters or annual holidays, may well be between 1 and 2 or even more. This means that when a person's income rises by 10 per cent, his food or calorie intake may rise by 5 per cent but his demand for TV sets, bicycles, scooters and holidays may rise by 10–20 per cent or more. Thus, if poverty estimates are pegged to calorie or food consumption, these fail to capture the rapid improvements that go on in terms of consumption and usage of various other goods and services such as the items mentioned above. In other words, food- and calorie-based estimates fail to reflect a population's actual improvement, especially the improvements in non-food terms, and to that extent exaggerate poverty. This inherent weakness of absolute and proportionate poverty estimates warrants serious recognition.

Yet another difficulty with poverty estimates based on calorie intake, food consumption and even personal income and expenditure information is that these data, which are the main source of poverty estimates in many countries of the world, do not take into account the benefits that come to people through the consumption of goods and services provided by the state and other agencies and are not included in purely personal expenditures and in personal expenditure surveys. India's National Sample Survey is a good example of one of the most thorough and, hence, most reliable personal expenditure surveys. But even in this survey, the benefits that are received by populations in terms of literacy programs, primary, middle and high school education, technical education and even college education, and also the benefits received in terms of state health and medical facilities, are totally omitted. In other words, in many countries millions of people obtain their education, technical education, higher education, primary health and medical supplies, not through their own expenditure but through public expenditure by the state. Many of these items are supplied entirely free without any cost to the public or at a heavily subsidized cost. In cases where the value of such public goods and services, entirely or substantially subsidized, constitutes a high proportion of total benefits received by the public, the estimates based merely on personal income or expenditure under-estimate the total benefits by a large margin. Strictly speaking, one would have to add to personal incomes or expenditures all those items of the central, state and local government budgets which provide public goods and services to the population, in order to arrive at a reasonable assessment of the number or proportion of the poor. This means that if the value of public goods and services is added to personal expenditure, a large number of people would go above the poverty line emanating merely from personal expenditures. That is to say, absolute and proportionate poverty might well be unnecessarily over-estimated in all these cases where public goods and services constitute a substantial proportion of personal benefits.

In a subsequent chapter (Chapter 6), the reader will notice that we have made an attempt to estimate the absolute number as well as the percentage of the poor according to calorie intake or income/expenditure. But, knowing the weakness of this method described above, we have also attempted to estimate the government budget expenditure on public goods and services, such as literacy, education and health in order to know their magnitudes and to see what difference this might make to public welfare and to the reduction of poverty.

Briefly, this work focuses not only on a statistical presentation of the numbers and the proportion of the poor in the aggregate and in some sectors of various types of economies at two points of time in recent years, but also on an economic analysis of the nature of poverty as well as the causes of poverty in different regimes and different epochs in the last two hundred years. Apart from statistical magnitudes, it is important to diagnose the causalty of poverty so that solutions and remedies are found to treat the causes rather than the symptoms. This book also examines the efforts and policies to get rid of poverty carried out by different economic regimes in the nineteenth and twentieth centuries and reflects on the successes and failures in meeting that objective. Five types of regimes are analysed for this purpose – the laissez-faire type of market economy, the welfare state, the planned (command) economies of the communist variety, the mixed economies of under-developed countries which, more recently, have adopted some semblance of economic planning, and the developing economies which have adopted structural adjustment programmes in a shift to market orientation. The analysis is thus spread over two centuries but the research itself is confined to various estimates of poverty at two points of time in recent years.

5 Some Macro-Indicators of Poverty

Of the various methods of poverty assessment, we take up first some macro-indicators. An assessment of overall poverty or affluence of different countries in each designated category can be made on the basis of broad indicators of income, consumption and investment. Income itself can be measured in many ways, the most commonly used definitions being the gross national product (GNP) and gross domestic product (GDP) in real terms – either in absolute or in per capita dimension.

1. GROSS NATIONAL PRODUCT (GNP)

Table 5.1 presents the magnitude of GNP in real terms for the selected countries: Columns 1 and 2 show the GNP per capita for 1994 and the average annual growth rate during 1985–94, respectively. The data reveal that:

(i) Among the highly industrialized countries, the developed market economies of Group 1 enjoy a substantially higher income as compared to all other groups including the planned economies of Group 2. The GNP per capita of the five selected developed market economies in terms of Purchasing Power Poverty (PPP) estimates ranges from US$ 25,880 for the USA to US$ 17,970 for the UK. This last and lowest figure among developed nations is three times higher than the highest GNP per capita of $6080 for Hungary and six times higher than the lowest figure of $2810 for Kazakhstan in the same group.

(ii) Within the planned economies themselves, the per capita GNP in Hungary is 100 per cent higher than in Kazakhstan.

(iii) The developing market economies of Group 3 in terms of PPP dollars have a range of per capita GNP from $21,900 (Singapore) to $3600 (Indonesia) and some of them are close to or even higher than the level of developed market economies.

(iv) The GNP per capita of the mixed economies of Group 4 ranges, among selected countries, from $5400 for Brazil to $1280 for India, the higher number being a multiple of more than four compared to

Table 5.1
Real GNP Per Capita and Annual Growth Rate

Country	GNP per capita ($) 1994	Avg. annual growth (%) 1985–94	PPP est. of GNP per capita ($) 1994
	(1)	(2)	(3)
1. Developed market economies			
USA	25 880	1.3	25 880
Japan	34 630	3.2	21 140
Australia	18 000	1.2	18 120
Germany	25 580	2.1	19 480
UK	18 340	1.3	17 970
2. Planned economies			
Hungary	3 840	(−)1.2	6 080
Poland	2 410	0.8	5 480
Russian Federation	2 650	(−)4.1	4 610
Kazakhstan	1 160	(−)6.5	2 810
Ukraine	1 910	(−)8.0	2 620
3. Developing market economies			
Korea	8 260	7.8	10 330
Singapore	22 500	6.1	21 900
Malaysia	3 480	5.6	8 440
Indonesia	880	6.0	3 600
Saudi Arabia	7 050	(−)1.7	9 480
4. Mixed economies			
Brazil	2 970	(−)0.4	5 400
China	530	7.8	2 510
Pakistan	430	1.3	2 130
India	320	2.9	1 280
Kenya	250	0.0	1 310
5. Least developed economies			
Bangladesh	220	2.0	1 330
Cambodia	–	–	–
Ethiopia	100	–	430
Niger	230	(−)2.1	770

Source: *World Development Report* (1996).

the lowest. Pakistan has a higher GNP per capita ($2130) compared to India, and China has an even higher per capita income of $2510.

Comparing the mixed economies with the developing market economies, with the exception of Brazil, all the other mixed economies have per capita GNP lower than in the developing market economies. The weakest performer, Indonesia, has a per capita GNP higher than all the other selected mixed economies except Brazil. But Korea, among the Group 3 countries, has a GNP per capita nearly three times larger than Indonesia's. Singapore seems to be an exception in this category having a per capita income of $21,900 – more than twice as much as the high-performing Korean economy.

(v) The selected LDCs of Group 5 have GNP per capita ranging from $1330 for Bangladesh – slightly higher than India's – to $430 for Ethiopia; and that latter figure is only one-third as much as for Bangladesh.

It is noteworthy and should be emphasized that GNP or GDP growth rates per capita are far from being identical with poverty lines. If, by any chance, the GNP/GDP per capita levels were equal to the poverty levels of income or product, a rise in GNP/GDP per capita itself could have been regarded as a marginal shift of a population from below to above the poverty line. In other words, a rise in per capita incomes would have been the same as a fall in the poverty proportion of population. That, however, is not the case and the shifts in per capita incomes do not necessarily reflect opposite shifts in the poverty population. That is why a GNP or GDP per capita index cannot be regarded as the dividing line between poverty and non-poverty.

Nevertheless, it seems most probable that when GNP/GDP per capita increases, poverty proportion decreases and vice versa. It is difficult to maintain, though not inconceivable, that a community becomes richer (in terms of GNP/GDP) by 10 per cent while at the same time the poverty proportion flares up. The best hypothesis seems to be that considerable increases in per capita GNP or GDP go hand-in-hand with decreases in poverty – and that decreases in the former spell an increase in the latter. In other words, the *direction* of change in GDP/GNP per capita and the poverty proportion is generally opposite, and thus the process of measuring the changing fortunes of society in terms of changes in average per capita GNP or GDP (though not the exact poverty proportion) becomes meaningful. It turns out, after all, that changes in GNP and GDP per capita are measures which indicate the *direction* of shifts in the poverty levels fairly well, even if they do not actually define poverty levels.

Focusing on changes over time and judging by the annual average growth rates of GDP per capita, we note that the developed market economies of Group 1 no longer have real GDP growth rates of 6 per cent and 5 per cent per annum in 1990–4 as they used to have earlier. The GDP growth rates per capita of the advanced market economies range from 4.1 per cent for Japan to 2.2 per cent for Germany – economies which in the 1960s staged a miracle in economic performance. In that past era while Japan had registered as high as a 10 per cent GDP growth rate for more than a decade, Germany too had consistently enjoyed 5–6 per cent growth for a prolonged period during the era of 'economic miracle'. However, it is clear that economic maturity has got the better of the advanced market economies and hence in the present phase the growth rates of GDP are both low and declining. A comparison of Columns 4 and 5 in Table 5.2 (page 64) shows that each of the developing market economies has a lower average growth rate in 1990–4 compared to the average of 1980–90. It is true that the number of years used for striking the average is larger in the 1980s than in the 1990s. But, it may be noted that both averages have a recessionary period of four years included within them. It is thus not an accident that USA should have moved from a growth rate of 3.0 to 2.5, Japan from 4.1 to 2.1, Australia from 3.5 to 3.4, Germany from 2.2 to 1.1 and UK from 3.2 to 0.8. This consistent dip tells a tale, perhaps, of secular decline or stagnation.

For the planned economies of Group 2, the period 1980–90 was not one of impressive growth rates of GDP per capita. None of the selected countries achieved even a 2 per cent growth rate in the decade 1980–90; but it is startling that all of them, except Poland, moved into negative growth rates: −2.0 per cent for Hungary; −0.6 for the Russian Federation, −14.4 for Ukraine and −14.3 for Khazakhstan. It appears that the transition from a planned economy to a market economy has not come easily in the erstwhile command economies, and frictions and maladjustments have dealt a body-blow to the growth rates during the transition. While the public sector enterprise has become discredited, the private sector has not been able to take its place in full substitution or a better performance. The transition, in other words, has been neither here nor there, and half-way houses and disincentive-oriented arrangements seem to have stultified the performance of the economies.

The mixed economies of Asia and Latin America have been doing fairly well in terms of per capita GNP growth, throughout the 1980s and in the early 1990s. China, in particular, has been a star performer with 10.2 per cent growth in the 1980s and 12.9 per cent in the 1990s. Pakistan and India have been plodding along, though the growth of the former has declined from 6.3 to 4.6 per cent while that of India has come down from 5.8 to 3.8 per cent. However, India's low figure during 1990–4 is explained by the inclusion of the crisis years 1990 and 1991. Once these are removed, the Indian figures rise substantially and convincingly. Brazil, however, showed a low as well as a declining GNP growth – from 2.7 to 2.2 per cent – and

Kenya registered a sharp decline from 4.2 to 0.9 per cent between the two time periods.

Among the least developed economies, while Bangladesh maintained a rate of 4.3 and 4.2 per cent in the years in question, Niger had a negative growth in both decades (−1.1 and −0.3 per cent).

2. GROSS DOMESTIC PRODUCT (GDP)

The Gross Domestic Product (GDP) is a national summing-up of all income transactions in a given year, excluding foreign transactions. Absolute and per capita estimates of GDP in real terms can be used as indicators of the level of prosperity. Comparison of real GDP in absolute or per capita terms between nations can be a rough measure of international differences in prosperity. Within a country, the changes in real GDP absolute or per capita can reflect the changes over time in average prosperity, positive or negative.

Table 5.3 gives the real GDP per capita (in purchasing power parity dollars) for 1985 and 1993. It will be observed that the GDP per capita levels and relative levels between countries are approximately the same as the GNP levels described earlier in Table 5.1. In Table 5.2 Columns 2 and 3 show the long-term (1980–90) and short-term (1990–4) rate of growth of GDP. Likewise, Columns 4 and 5, depicting what is called the GDP deflator, indicates the extent of erosion in real value of production due to a rise in prices. The following may be noted:

- As compared to the average annual growth rate for the decade (1980–90), the rate has generally decelerated for the Group 1 in the period 1990–4. The corresponding growth rates for the planned economies (Group 2) has worsened from less than 2 per cent per annum growth of GDP to negative growth rates of a high order. The GDP deflator accordingly shows unprecedented high rates of increase in prices.
- The developing market economies (Group 3) are also seen to improve upon their performance in the early nineties over the previous decade, 1980–90, which was also an era of high growth for them. The increase in prices was low and restrained within a single digit. The mixed economies (Group 4) however, showed a divergent trend, except China which continued to improve its performance in GDP growth rate.
- The least developed economies (Group 5) showed either a low growth rate of GDP or a declining trend i.e. a negative rate of change.

Table 5.2
Growth Rate of Real GDP, Gross Domestic Investment and Private Consumption Expenditure

Country	Real GDP growth		GDP deflator		Gross domestic investment		Pvt. consumption expenditure
	1980–90	1990–94	1980–90	1990–94	1980–90	1990–94	1980–93
(1)	(2)	(3)	(4)	(5)	(6)	(7)	(8)
1. Developed market economies							
USA	3.0	2.5	4.1	2.4	3.4	4.1	2.9
Japan	4.1	1.2	1.5	1.1	5.7	(–)0.4	3.5
Australia	3.5	3.4	7.3	1.2	2.6	0.9	3.2
Germany	2.2	1.1	2.6	3.8	2.0	(–)1.8	2.6
UK	3.2	0.8	5.7	4.0	6.4	(–)2.0	3.3
2. Planned economies							
Hungary	1.6	(–)2.0	8.6	22.4	(–)0.4	3.2	0.0
Poland	1.7	1.6	53.9	36.9	0.9	(–)3.3	1.6
Russian Federation	1.9	(–)10.6	3.2	616.7	–	–	(–)3.5
Kazakhstan	1.5	(–)14.3	2.8	976.5	1.9	(–)26.0	2.4
Ukraine	–	(–)14.4	–	1 169.1	–	–	1.5
3. Developing market economies							
Korea	9.4	6.6	5.9	6.3	11.9	4.3	8.6
Singapore	6.4	8.3	2.0	3.7	3.7	6.1	6.3
Malaysia	5.2	8.4	1.7	3.7	2.6	14.9	5.5
Indonesia	6.1	7.6	8.5	7.4	7.0	7.5	4.4
Saudi Arabia	(–)1.2	1.9	(–)3.7	0.4	–	–	–

4. Mixed economies

Brazil	2.7	2.2	284.5	1231.5	0.2	1.8	1.8
China	10.2	12.9	5.8.	10.8	11.0	15.4	7.9
Pakistan	6.3	4.6	6.7	10.8	5.9	4.7	4.8
India	5.8	3.8	8.0	10.1	6.5	1.2	4.7
Kenya	4.2	0.9	9.0	17.7	0.8	(−)2.2	4.7

5. Least developed economies

Bangladesh	4.3	4.2	9.5	4.1	1.4	4.7	2.7
Cambodia	–	–	–	–	–	–	–
Ethiopia	2.3	–	3.4	–	–	–	–
Niger	(−)1.1	(−)0.3	2.9	4.7	(−)5.9	(−)6.9	(−)0.2

Source: World Development Report, 1996, The World Bank.

Table 5.3
Real GDP Per Capita (PPP$)

Country	1985*	1993
1. Developed market economies		
USA	19 850	24 680
Japan	13 650	20 660
Australia	14 530	18 530
Germany	13 388	18 840
UK	13 060	17 230
2. Planned economies		
Hungary	5 920	6 059
Poland	4 190	4 702
Russian Federation		4 760
Kazakhstan	6 270**	3 710
Ukraine		3 250
3. Developing market economies		
Korea	5 680	9 710
Singapore	10 540	19 350
Malaysia	5 070	8 360
Indonesia	1 820	3 270
Saudi Arabia	9 350	12 600
4. Mixed economies		
Brazil	4 620	5 500
China	2 470	2 330
Pakistan	1 790	2 160
India	870	1 240
Kenya	1 010	1 400
5. Least developed economies		
Bangladesh	720	1 290
Cambodia	1 000	1 250
Ethiopia	350	420
Niger	610	790

* Refers to 1985–8.
** USSR.
Source: *Human Development Report* issue for 1991 and 1996,
UNDP.

3. GROSS DOMESTIC INVESTMENT

Columns 6 and 7 of Table 5.2 show the rate of change in domestic investment which indicates the relative efforts made in different countries to
accelerate the pace of development. The following broad conclusions
emerge.

- As compared to the previous decade, 1980–90, the rate of gross investment has generally declined in Group 1 economies, except in the US, and a negative growth rate for some economies has been recorded during the early 1990s. For the planned economies of Group 2, the investment situation is even more grim and has deteriorated at a faster pace, ranging from 1 to 8 per cent per annum.
- The developing market economies (Group 3) were generally able to enhance the rate of gross investment but the corresponding rate for mixed economies (Group 4), except for China, has declined. The least developed economies of Group 5 show a very low rate of investment whereas Niger shows continuing deterioration in the rate of gross domestic investment.

4. PRIVATE CONSUMPTION EXPENDITURE

The rate of change in private consumption expenditure indicates the extent of improvement in the well-being of people. Column 8 shows the long-term change (1980–93) in the rate of private consumption expenditure.

- The Group 1 countries generally recorded a steady improvement in the rate of increase in consumption expenditure. The planned economies, Group 2, showed a dismal record as the improvement was either negligible or negative.
- The developing countries, both market economies and mixed economies, generally showed a higher rate of increase of consumption expenditures.

Thus, the long-term trend of increase in private consumption expenditure indicates an impressive improvement for developing economies and a steady rise for the advanced countries. However, the socialist countries suffered a deterioration in the levels of consumption expenditure and the overall situation in the least developed economies also remained depressive.

6 Absolute and Proportionate Poverty

In almost all the countries, the absolute number and the share of population living below the country-specific poverty line have been declining. Some countries have, however, been more successful than others in annihilating poverty as the extent of the decline in poverty ratio widely differs across the developing world. What obstructs or facilitates poverty reduction is a matter for a separate discussion elsewhere in this book. The evidence presented in Tables 6.1 and 6.2 is self-revealing and demonstrates that the incidence of poverty, as defined by the countries themselves, is tending to diminish in terms of both absolute number and the proportion of poor people to the total population. While Table 6.1 depicts the poverty scenario for a few countries till the 1980s, Table 6.2 shows the recent picture for the early 1990s which will be briefly discussed below.

Table 6.2 presents the relevant data pertaining to the absolute and proportionate level of poverty for different countries. Such data for the developed market economies and the planned economies are not provided/published by international agencies such as the UNDP and the World Bank. The presentation here, therefore, is confined to the countries of Groups 3, 4 and 5 only.

- Columns 2 and 3 show the absolute number of persons in poverty in 1990 and 1992 for the total and the rural population. In almost all the countries there is a reduction in the number of people in poverty. The absolute number of such people is very low for the developing market economies while their number is substantial in the mixed economies and the least developed economies.
- The poverty ratio, that is the ratio of people in poverty to the total population, which may also be termed proportionate poverty, is shown in columns 4, 5 and 6 for the total, rural and urban populations, respectively. As noted earlier, compared to the developing market economies, the poverty ratios are significantly higher for the mixed and the least developed economies. Whereas the poverty percentage for the developing market economies varies between 5 per cent for Korea and 25 per cent for Indonesia, the corresponding figures for the mixed economies vary between 9 per cent for China and 52 per cent for Kenya. This percentage for India was 40 in 1990 while for the poorest of the LDCs,

Table 6.1
Changes in Country-Specific Poverty Line
(Based on expenditure per household member)

Country	Head count index				Number of poor			
	Early year	*Per cent*	*Last year*	*Per cent*	*Early year*	*Per cent*	*Last year*	*Per cent*
(1)	(2)	(3)	(4)	(5)	(6)	(7)	(8)	(9)
Developing market economies								
Singapore	1972	31	1982	10	1972	0.7	1982	0.2
Malaysia	1973	37	1987	15	1973	4.1	1987	2.2
	1984	15	1987	14	1984	2.3	1987	2.2
Indonesia	1970	–	1987	17	1970	67.9	1987	30
	1984	28	1987	17	1984	45.4	1987	30
Mixed economies								
Brazil	1960	50	1980	21	1960	36.1	1980	25.4
	1981	19	1987	24	1981	23.1	1987	33.2
China	1985	10	1988	14	1985	79.2	1988	101.3
Pakistan	1962	54	1984	–	1962	26.5	1984	21.3
India	1972	54	1983	43	1972	311.4	1983	315.0
	1977	50	1983	43	1977	324.9	1983	315.0

Note: This table uses country-specific poverty lines and is based on expenditure per household member. In some cases, the poverty line has been set at 30 per cent of mean income or expenditure. The range of poverty lines, expressed in terms of expenditure per household member and in PPP dollars, was approximately $300–700 a year in May 1985, except for Malaysia ($1420) and Singapore ($860).
The head count index is the percentage of the population below the poverty line. The average income shortfall is the mean distance of consumption or income of the poor below the poverty line, as a proportion of the poverty line.
Source: *World Development Report*, 1990, the World Bank, pp. 41 and 43, Tables 3.2 and 3.3.

namely Bangladesh and Ethiopia, it was as high as 78 and 60 per cent, respectively.

- It is also clear that poverty is concentrated in the rural areas of most countries.
- To alleviate the incidence of poverty, almost every country has undertaken social security measures to protect the poorest of the poor. Column 7 indicates the expenditure on social security benefits as a share of GDP. The developed economies spend as high as 16.2 per cent of GDP on social security. The corresponding ratio for the developing countries is very low and varies greatly across the groups and countries, as may be observed in Table 6.2.

The Poverty of Nations

Table 6.2
Absolute and Proportionate Poverty

Country	People in absolute poverty, 1992		Poverty ratio (%)			Social security benefit exp. (%) of GDP, 1994
	Total (m.)	*Rural (m.)*	*Total*	*Rural*	*Urban*	
(1)	(2)	(3)	(4)	(5)	(6)	(7)
1. Developed market economies						
Korea	2.1	0.5	5	4	5	7.5
	(7.0)	(1.3)				
Singapore	–	–	–	–	–	7.1
Malaysia	3.0	2.3	16.0	22	8	0.5
	(4.7)	(3.8)				
Indonesia	47.8	35.9	25	27	20	–
	(69.5)	(55.2)				
Saudi Arabia	–	–	–	–	–	1.4
2. Mixed economies						
Brazil	72.4	25.9	47	73	38	4.6
	(–)	(–)		(–)		
China	105.0	105.0	9	13	–	3.4
	(–)	(75.6)				
Pakistan	35.0	24.3	28	29	26	–
	(36.8)	(24.5)				
India	350.0	270.0	40	42	33	0.5
	(410.0)	(320.0)				
Kenya	13.2	10.4	52	55	10	0.6
	(11.2)	(10.6)				
3. Least developed economies						
Bangladesh	93.2	84.3	78	86	–	2.1
	(99.4)	(83.1)				
Cambodia	–	–	–	–	–	–
Ethiopia	31.9	29.3	60	63	–	1.4
	(30.1)	(26.5)				
Niger	–	2.3	–	35	–	0.3
		(2.0)				

Note: Figures in parenthesis in Cols 2 and 3 relate to 1990.

Table 6.3
Availability of Food

Country	Food production per capita index 1979–81 = 100 1992	Daily calorie supply 1992	Food import as % merchandise import 1992 (1970)
(1)	(2)	(3)	(4)
1. Developing market economies			
Korea	99	3 298	6(17)
Singapore	49	–	6(16)
Malaysia	187	2 884	7(22)
Indonesia	144	2 756	6(12)
Saudi Arabia	–	2 751	16(28)
2. Mixed economies			
Brazil	116	2 824	9(11)
China	142	2 729	5(7)
Pakistan	115	2 316	15(2)
India	125	2 395	5(21)
Kenya	94	2 075	–
3. Least developed economies			
Bangladesh	97	2 091	16(23)
Cambodia	136	2 021	–
Ethiopia	86	1 610	15(9)
Niger	85	2 257	17(14)

Source: *Human Development Report*, 1995, UNDP.

AVAILABILITY OF FOOD

Table 6.3 provides an indication of food availability in different countries. The following may be observed.

Index of Food Production (per Capita)

Column 2 presents the index of per capita food production with the base as 1979–81 = 100. This demonstrates the extent of improvement in per capita food production. The experience of different countries is quite mixed as there are those which have considerably increased the level of production while some others have recorded a poor performance.

Daily Calorie Supply (per Capita)

Daily calorie supply per capita is generally higher for the developing market economies – 3298 for Korea and 2884 for Malaysia – as compared to the mixed economies – China 2729 and Pakistan 2316. The corresponding figures for the least developed countries are very low in comparison with an average of 2100 calories prescribed as a minimum by the World Bank. The figure for India is 2395 calories per capita per day in Group 4 while Brazil and Kenya in the same category of mixed economies have 2824 and 2075 calories per person per day, respectively.

Food Import (as Percentage of Merchandise Import)

A comparison at two points of time (i.e. 1970 and 1992) shows that food dependency ratio (the ratio of food imports to food consumption) for most countries has substantially declined. The comparison of countries across the Groups is quite mixed but it does indicate that in the least developed economies the dependency ratio has increased, especially for Ethiopia and Niger. This ratio has substantially declined from 21 per cent for India in 1970 to 5 per cent in 1992. Among all the countries here, India and China are least dependent on the import of food (5 per cent of the total merchandise import). The index of production of food and calorie supply per capita are, however, higher for China as compared to India. It emerges that the incidence of poverty is being reduced everywhere and this process is somewhat faster in developing market economies. The LDCs are, however, still in the grip of a high level of poverty, a situation requiring strong interventions through relevant policies and programmes to ensure a decent standard of living for people.

7 Sectoral Poverty: Literacy, Education and Health

Having examined some overall and aggregative aspects of national poverty, we proceed to assess sectoral poverty within national boundaries in terms of achievement and lack of it in the areas of social services, mainly education and health care. Different sectoral indicators of physical attainments and financial allocations are analysed in order to gain an idea of the extent of deprivation in different countries and across groups of countries.

LEVELS OF EDUCATIONAL ATTAINMENT

Some sets of indicators have been identified, as in Table 7.1, which reveal the level of educational attainments for different countries. Data are presented for two points of time – 1987 and 1992 – for which information is available for selected variables. The results indicate the following.

Adult Literacy

The literacy rate refers to the percentage of people aged 15 and above who can, with understanding, both read and write a short, simple statement about their everyday life. As an indicator of basic human needs, which is provided almost free by every country, the literacy rate and/or absolute number of illiterate persons, lend perspective on the overall educational development of a country. In this context, Columns 2 and 3 of Table 7.1 demonstrate the literacy rate and the absolute number of illiterate persons respectively. The following observations may be made:

1. All the countries in Group 1 and some in Group 2 have a literacy rate as high as 99 per cent, in 1992, while the remaining countries in the Group 2 are very close to the levels attained by the countries in Group 1, which indicate almost complete liquidation of illiteracy in the developed market economies and planned economies.
2. In Group 3, Indonesia with 82.5 per cent literacy, has the highest number of illiterate persons – 20.6 million. All other countries in the Group have

Table 7.1
Levels of Educational Attainments

Country	Adult literacy Rate 1992	Illiterates age 15 years and above m. 1992	Mean years of schooling 1992	Percentage of age groups in education Primary 1987	Primary 1992	Secondary 1987	Secondary 1992	Tertiary 1987	Tertiary 1992	Primary net enrolment 1987	Primary net enrolment 1992	Primary pupil teacher ratio 1987	Primary pupil teacher ratio 1992	Scientists & technicians (per 1000 people) 1988–92
(1)	(2)	(3)	(4)	(5)	(6)	(7)	(8)	(9)	(10)	(11)	(12)	(13)	(14)	(15)
1. Developed market economies														
USA	99.0	–	12.4	100	104	91	–	60	76	–	98	25	–	55*
Japan	99.0	–	10.8	102	102	96	–	28	32	–	100	–	20	110*
Australia	99.0	–	12.0	106	107	83	82	22	40	–	98	–	17	48*
Germany	99.0	–	11.6	103	107	94	–	30	36	–	89	–	16	86*
UK	99.0	–	11.7	106	104	83	86	22	28	–	97	–	–	90*
2. Planned economies														
Hungary	99.0	–	9.8	97	89	70	81	15	15	95	86	14	12	50*
Poland	99.0	–	8.2	101	83	80	83	18	23	99	96	16	17	164*
Russian Federation	98.7	–	9.0	–	98	–	–	–	–	–	–	–	–	–
Kazakhstan	97.5	–	5.0	–	–	–	–	–	–	–	–	–	–	–
Ukraine	95.0	–	6.0	–	–	–	–	–	–	–	–	–	–	–

3. Developed market economies

Korea	97.4	0.8	9.3	101	105	88	90	36	42	99	100	37	32	2.3
Singapore	89.9	0.2	4.0	–	107	59	58	7	7	–	100	–	30	1.8
Malaysia	81.5	2.0	5.6	102	93	46	38	–	7	–	–	22	20	0.4
Indonesia	82.5	20.6	4.1	118	115	44	46	–	10	–	97	–	23	–
Saudi Arabia	60.6	3.7	3.9	71	78	44	46	13	14	–	64	22	14	–

4. Mixed economies

Brazil	81.9	17.7	4.0	103	106	39	39	11	12	84	86	–	23	–
China	79.3	73.6	5.0	132	121	43	51	2	2	98	96	–	22	1.6
Pakistan	35.7	43.8	1.9	52	46	19	21	5	–	–	–	41	41	0.1
India	49.9	271.8	2.4	98	102	39	44	–	–	–	–	–	63	0.3
Kenya	74.5	3.1	2.3	96	95	23	29	1	2	–	–	–	31	–

5. Least developed economies

Bangladesh	36.4	40.0	2.0	59	77	18	19	5	4	53	69	48	63	–
Cambodia	–	–	2.0	–	–	–	–	1	–	–	–	–	–	–
Ethopia	28.9	17.3	0.3	22	37	15	12	1	1	27	–	–	27	–
Niger	12.4	3.5	0.2	29	29	6	6	1	–	–	25	–	38	–

Source: Human Development Report, UNDP (various issues).
Note: *Figures relate to 1986–90.

about three million or fewer illiterate people who could be made
literate within a short span of time.

3. The mixed economies of Group 4 show a divergent situation. For
   instance, while Brazil with 81.9 per cent literacy rate has 17.6 million
   illiterate population, the corresponding figures for India are 50 per cent
   and 271.8 million. China and Kenya have a literacy rate as high as 79.3
   and 74.5 per cent respectively, while the corresponding absolute numbers are 173.6 and 3.1 million. In this Group, Pakistan has the lowest
   literacy rate of 35.7 per cent involving 43.8 million people. The number of illiterates in India at 271.8 million exceeds the total number of
   illiterates in all the countries under reference in this study.

4. Literacy rates for countries in Group 5 are the lowest, as may be expected,
   and range between 36.4 per cent for Bangladesh and 12.4 per cent for
   Niger. The countries in this Group, as also in Group 4, need to make
   concerted efforts to improve the access to educational facilities and to
   promote adult literacy.

Mean Years of Schooling, 1992

Given the wide variations in the quality of education across the countries,
mean years of schooling is the single indicator which reflects the level
of educational attainments in different countries. As one goes down the
ladder from Group 1 to Group 5 countries, the figure for mean years of
schooling keeps declining – reflecting an insufficiency or poverty of educational attainments. This indicator shows that for industrialized countries
mean years of schooling is the highest in the range of 11 to 12 years for
countries of Group 1, but varies for Group 2 countries in the range of 5 to
9 years. It also varies widely for other groups of countries.

In the developing countries, mean years of schooling is generally higher
for market-oriented economies than for mixed economies. For India, the
figures for mean years of schooling turns out to be as low as 2.4 years
whereas the corresponding figures for Korea and China are 9.3 and 5 years,
respectively. The figure is abysmally low for the LDCs in Group 5 and
varies between 0.2 years for Niger to 2 years for Bangladesh.

Enrolment Ratio: Primary, Secondary and Tertiary Levels

The ratio of young people enrolled in primary, secondary and tertiary education, without differentiating between these three levels, is yet another
indicator of educational improvement. Columns 5 to 10 in Table 7.1 reveal

the levels of enrolment at different stages of education. Data show relatively higher levels of educational achievements for countries in Group 1 and 2. The developing countries, particularly the mixed economies, and the LDCs are lagging far behind the economically better-off countries.

Specifically, the data reveal that the enrolment ratio at primary level has generally been above 100 per cent for Group 1 and for some countries, namely Korea, Singapore and Indonesia, in Group 3, and Brazil, China and India, in Group 4. For all other countries, the ratio is less than 100 per cent. This ratio has marginally deteriorated for the countries in Group 2 and for Pakistan (Group 4) during the period 1987 to 1992. The least developed economies in Group 5 have the lowest enrolment ratio, 29 and 37 per cent for Niger and Ethiopia, respectively.

Likewise, enrolment ratios for secondary and tertiary levels of education are considerably higher for Group 1 as compared to other Groups. Inter-country differences are, however, glaring with respect to tertiary level education and the ratio varies within and across the Groups. For instance, in Group 1, the enrolment ratio for tertiary level is as low as 28 per cent for UK and as high as 76 per cent for USA. The corresponding ratios for Malaysia and Korea, in Group 3, are 7 and 42 per cent, respectively. The enrolment ratio, already high, has generally improved in Group 1 economies except perhaps for the UK, but shows a two-way movement in other groups, between 1987 and 1992. That educational poverty is not being annihilated rapidly but is generally 'sticky' is evident from the data in Table 7.1.

The student–teacher ratio for advanced countries is much lower than the ratios obtained in developing countries and reflects wide variations in the quality of education in developed and developing countries. In Groups 1 and 2 an average teacher handles a small-sized class of 12 to 20 students (column 9), while the size of the average class increases substantially in other Groups. Pakistan, India, Kenya, Bangladesh and Niger have average student concentrations of 41, 63, 31, 63 and 27, respectively, to be attended to by one teacher.

Availability of Science and Technology Manpower

Science and Technology (S&T) has a significant bearing on productivity and economic development. Column15 shows the number of S&T manpower per 1000 people, and reveals that the countries in Groups 1 and 2 have significantly higher S&T manpower ratio in the range of 48 for Australia to 164 for Poland as compared to developing and least developed countries of Groups 4 and 5 (for instance 0.1 for Pakistan, 2.3 for

Korea and 0.3 for India). This difference is glaring and indicates the long distance which the developing and least developed countries have yet to travel towards industrial and scientific achievement and hence closer to self-sufficiency in S&T manpower and an effective management of technology.

Public Expenditure on Education

We can get an idea about educational efforts, as measured in terms of public expenditure on education, from data relating to educational expenditure in relation to GNP and total public expenditure (Table 7.2). It turns out that the level of investment in education has been much higher in developed countries, above 5 per cent of GNP, compared to others, and that explains, among other things, the higher levels of physical attainment in terms of GNP, GDP and investment in the critical sectors of the developed economies, as shown above. Some of the developing countries, namely Malaysia, Saudi Arabia and Kenya, are devoting a major share of income to educational development, between 3 and 6 per cent, which compares favourably with advanced countries. There are, however, considerable differences within the groups and across the groups in the allocation of funds for development of human resources through education.

FACILITIES FOR HEALTH CARE

Good health or lack of it is an important component of the quality of life of a people. Efforts made by different countries to provide health-care facilities are reflected in life expectancy at birth. Relevant indicators such as the share of national income spent on health-improving activities, namely provision for hospitals, doctors and nurses, show the extent of efforts being made in attacking health poverty. Table 7.3 presents the relevant data about life expectancy, health, health-care facilities and the percentage of GDP spent on health.

Life Expectancy

A higher life expectancy is not the result of health measures alone. Higher per capita income, higher literacy and better education and awareness as well as other factors have an impact on life expectancy. Though there are considerable differences in life expectancy across the countries, people in the industrialized world – developed market economies as well as planned economies – live a relatively longer life, above 70 years as compared to

Table 7.2
Public Expenditure on Education

Country	Public expenditure on education 1990		
	as % of GNP	as % of total govt expenditure	Primary & secondary education (as % of all levels)
(1)	(2)	(3)	(4)
1. Developed market economies			
USA	5.5	1.8	–
Japan	3.5	–	–
Australia	5.5	7.0	–
Germany	5.4	–	–
UK	5.3	13.2	–
2. Planned economies			
Hungary	6.2	3.3	–
Poland	4.9	–	–
Russian Federation	–	–	–
Kazakhstan	–	–	–
Ukraine	–	–	–
3. Developing market economies			
Korea	3.6	22.4	79
Singapore	3.4	–	65
Malaysia	6.9	18.8	76
Indonesia	–	–	–
Saudi Arabia	6.2	17.8	–
4. Mixed economies			
Brazil	4.6	–	56
China	2.3	12.4	67
Pakistan	3.4	–	70
India	3.5	11.2	71
Kenya	6.8	16.7	77
5. Least developed economies			
Bangladesh	2.0	10.3	88
Cambodia	–	–	–
Ethiopia	4.8	9.4	82
Niger	–	–	–

60 years or less in developing countries. This may be attributable *inter alia* to better health facilities as evident from the availability of doctors and nurses per 1000 population. Obviously, the advanced countries have succeeded in raising life expectancy (Column 1) and reducing the years of life lost due to premature death (Column 2). However, there is a perceptible rise in AIDS cases in advanced countries (Column 3).

Table 7.3
Some Statistics on Health, Health Care Facilities and Life Expectancy

Country	Life expectancy at birth (years) 1988	1993	Years of life lost prematurely per 1000 people 1990	AIDS cases per 100,000 people 1992	Population Per doctor 1984	1990	Per nurse 1984	1990	Nurses per doctor 1984	1990	Expenditure on health as per cent of GDP 1984	1990
(1)	(2)	(3)	(4)	(5)	(6)	(7)	(8)	(9)	(10)	(11)	(12)	(13)
1. Developed market economies												
USA	(76)	76	11	19.6	(470)	420	(70)	–	–	–	*(11.2)	13.3
Japan	(78)	80	8	0.2	(660)	610	(180)	–	–	–	*(6.8)	6.8
Australia	(76)	78	9	3.6	(440)	440	(110)	–	–	–	*(7.1)	8.6
Germany	(75)	76	12	2.1	(380)	370	(230)	–	–	–	*(8.2)	9.1
UK	(75)	76	12	2.2	–	710	(120)	–	–	–	*(6.1)	6.6
2. Planned economies												
Hungary	(70)	69	15	0.2	(310)	340	(170)	–	–	–	*(3.2)	6.0
Poland	(72)	71	16	0.1	(490)	490	(190)	–	–	–	*(4.0)	5.1
Russian Federation	–	65	–	–	–	–	–	–	–	–	*(3.2)	–
Kazakhstan	–	70	–	–	–	–	–	–	–	–	–	–
Ukraine	–	69	–	–	–	–	–	–	–	–	–	–

3. Developing market economies

Korea	71	(70)	10	–	(1 160)	1 370	(580)	1 370	–	–	1.0	6.6
Singapore	75	(74)	9	0.6	(1 310)	920	–	240	(1.0)	3.8	(1.3)	1.9
Malaysia	71	(70)	15	0.2	(1 930)	2 700	(1 010)	690	(1.9)	3.9	(1.8)	3.0
Indonesia	63	(61)	36	–	(460)	7 140	(1 260)	2 550	(7.5)	2.8	(0.7)	2.0
Saudi Arabia	70	(64)	37	–	(690)	660	(320)	1 040	(2.2)	0.6	(4.0)	4.8

4. Mixed economies

Brazil	67	(65)	26	4.8	(1 080)	670	(1 210)	6 700	(0.9)	0.1	(2.4)	4.2
China	69	(70)	–	–	(1 000)	730	(1 710)	1 460	(0.6)	0.5	(1.4)	3.5
Pakistan	62	(55)	61	–	(2 910)	2 940	(4 900)	1 720	(0.6)	1.7	(0.2)	3.4
India	61	(58)	–	–	(2 520)	2 440	(1 700)	2 220	(1.5)	1.1	(0.9)	3.5
Kenya	58	(59)	45	24.7	(9 970)	71 430	(950)	22 320	(10.5)	3.2	(1.7)	4.3

5. Least developed economies

Bangladesh	56	(51)	69	–	(6 730)	6 670	(8 980)	8 340	(0.7)	0.8	(0.6)	3.2
Cambodia	–	–	–	–	–	25 000	–	3 130	–	0.8	–	–
Ethiopia	48	(47)	107	5.5	(78 970)	33 330	(5 400)	13 890	(11.1)	2.4	(1.3)	–
Niger	47	(45)	121	3.8	(39 730)	33 330	(460)	2 950	(8.5)	11.3	(0.8)	5.0

Source: Human Development Report, UNDP (various issues).

Health Expenditure

Health expenditure as a percentage of GNP is considerably higher in industrialized countries, 6–13 per cent, in comparison with the developing
countries, about 3–4 per cent or less. Owing to income constraints poor
countries have been spending much less than the amounts required to
assure the necessary provision for health care.

8 Human Deprivation and Distress

The phenomenon of human deprivation and distress is found to be widespread in all the countries even though these are at different levels of socio-economic development. While millions of people in economically backward countries are deprived of basic needs like food, clothing, shelter, clean drinking water, sanitation and other amenities necessary for a decent living, a large number of people in advanced countries are distressed as a result of several problems which are essentially a by-product of industrialization, secular stagnation of mature economies, recurring recessions and rapid economic and social change in the post-development phase. These seem to result in unemployment, high crime rates, high divorce rates, drugs, drunkenness and new diseases. Table 8.1 demonstrates the nature and the extent of some of these phenomena which are significant causes of human distress. In spite of considerable success in augmenting economic opportunities, unemployment rates are observed to be very high both in the developed market economies and in the formerly planned economies. As seen in Table 8.1, the range is as high as 7 to 15 per cent in 1993. However, for some countries (for example Japan and the Russian Federation), unemployment was as low as 2.5 and 0.8 per cent, respectively, though this figure conceals a good deal of under-employment.

As elaborated in Chapter 11, it appears that the highly developed and industrial economies of North America, Western Europe, Australia, New Zealand and Japan have become a scene of economic maturity and capital saturation. Many high-tech industries like electronics, computerization, communications and information technologies are still expanding; but a large range of conventional lines from steel to housing and from railways to shipping, which account for a considerable proportion of the GNP, have been stagnating owing to secular forces. As a result, the growth rates of GNP in these mature economies have declined from 5 to 6 per cent in the early 1960s to less than 2 per cent in the 1990s. Recurring recessions have become a regular phenomenon, so much so that growth rates have dwindled to 1 per cent or even a negative figure during the recessions and to between 2 and 3 per cent during recoveries.

Moreover, either as a cause of sluggish growth or as a result of it, investment rates have generally declined. It is very possible that the huge capital stock of the industrialized economies, in the face of a slow-down of

Table 8.1
Unemployment Rate and Indicators of Human Deprivation

Country	Unemployment rate (%) 1993	Prisoners per 100 000 1990	Homicides per 1 000 000 1990	Drug crimes per 100 000	Adult rapes per 1000	Suicides per 100 000 1989–93	Injuries from road accidents per 100 000
(1)	(2)	(3)	(4)	(5)	(6)	(7)	(8)
1. Developed market economies							
USA	6.7	–	–	234	90.4	25	1398
Japan	2.5	38	1.6	31	1.8	33	640
Australia	10.9	84	–	403	2.3	22	169
Germany	8.2	–	6.8	–	–	32	660
UK	10.2	–	2.5	–	–	17	605
2. Planned economies							
Hungary	12.1	119	2.7	–	1.1	73	–
Poland	15.7	132	–	–	1.9	30	–
Russian Federation	0.8	–	–	–	–	65	–
Kazakhstan	1.0	–	4.0	–	–	44	–
Ukarine	–	–	–	–	–	39	–

Source: Human Development Report, 1995, UNDP.

aggregate demand (GNP), is leading to a decline in the rate of return to new investment – except in a few expanding lines – and this would seem to be an independent cause of decline in investment rates in relation to GDP.

The upshot of a slow-down in GNP growth and a decline in investment rates is clearly the emergence of large-scale unemployment, the rate of which is very high indeed. Unemployment is high both as a secular phenomenon and as a periodic occurrence in phases of recessions – and this becomes a crucial cause of human misery and deprivation.

Socio-economic crime rates are also inordinately high despite significant improvements in income, health facilities and levels of education. For the countries of the first and second worlds for which relevant data are available, Table 8.1 reveals the number of prisoners, homicides, drug-related crimes, adult rapes and suicides to be enormous, depicting a high level of human distress. Some of these adversities emerge from unemployment itself while others are independent phenomena with independent causes.

9 Levels of Human Development

Some of the previous chapters were concerned with the measurements of overall or aggregate poverty and others with segmental or sectoral poverty. This brings us to the latest attempt to evolve a measure of overall poverty based upon or derived from sectoral and some general estimates of richness and poverty such as income per capita, education and life expectancy. The aim of this exercise, conducted under the auspices of UNDP, is that despite a summing-up of these three measures, the weighting problem should be avoided in substantial measure. It is to be noted that while the income index is an overall index and the education index is a sectoral index (with wide overall implications), the life expectancy index is itself composed of several socio-economic factors such as health, information, medical facilities, education, literacy, income levels, and so on. While the human development index (HDI) evolved by the UNDP is certainly an improvement on the previous techniques of measuring richness or poverty, it cannot claim to be the last word on poverty estimates. For what it is worth – and it is worth a lot – we use the HDI in the present work for all the 24 countries for two points of time (1985 and 1992) as one of the best available indices of poverty and richness.

Four types of poverty have been described so far – (i) per capita GNP estimates, (ii) the absolute number of people below the poverty line, (iii) the percentage of people below the poverty line, and (iv) relative poverty of some groups or countries compared to others. These reflect the attempts to sum up the poverty or richness of different countries in a single figure for each type and country. These heroic attempts have their own merits especially in that they yield short-hand statements which can sum up a highly complex phenomenon in just one value. However, as we have seen, each one of these definitions of overall poverty, summed up in a single figure, has its own limitations and leaves something to be desired. This has led economists and social scientists to drop the idea of an overall poverty estimate in order to move on to more detailed poverty estimates for different sectors and segments of the economy. How would it be if, instead of an aggregated figure of average per capita income or per capita income below the poverty line, a society's wealth or poverty were measured in terms of literacy, education and health, and so on? It turns out that it should be possible to assess the poverty of literacy (the percentage of illiterates to literates), educational poverty (the percentage of uneducated – on some definition – to the educated), and health poverty (the percentage of the unhealthy population – on some definitions – to the healthy; that is to say the percentage of people without access to literary, education and health measures to those with such access. As in the case of average per capita income or per capita income below the poverty line, if estimates of sectoral poverty were made, it should be possible to reflect upon the *changes* in sectoral poverty between one point of time and another and the differences in sectoral poverty across nations, regions and categories – and changes in these differences over time.

Such sectoral or segmental estimates have their own hazards. On the whole, however, they are relatively easy and only require appropriate data-gathering through surveys and other mechanisms and the estimation of the required parameters.

Attempts have been made by some experts and some governments or world organizations to make separate poverty estimates for different sectors and then sum them up, for a given point in time or period of time, into an aggregate for all the sectors put together. This raises difficult issues, for example the need to attach different weights to different sectors and then add the sectoral figure into a single weighted average. This is virtually an impossible task as the weightage issue is almost insoluble. What weight can one attach to education *vis-à-vis* health and what weight to health *vis-à-vis* income or housing or transportation or communication? Many experts who have worked with sectoral estimates of poverty preferred to keep them and use them merely as sectoral estimates in order to avoid the weightage issue and the exercise of summing them up into a single all-sectors figure. In this way the problem becomes relatively manageable. In the present research, too, we prefer to use the sectoral estimates independently for each sector and would do so for all the 24 countries in our purposive sample at two points of time in order to reflect whether sectoral poverty has been increasing or decreasing and also whether the degree of poverty in one country or region is more than in another.

METHODOLOGY OF HUMAN DEVELOPMENT INDEX (HDI)

Human Development Index (HDI) is a composite index which attempts a master summing-up of the quality of life of a given population. HDI is computed on the basis of GNP per capita, life expectancy at birth and educational attainment of the population (as measured by a combined gross enrolment ratio for all educational levels, primary, secondary and tertiary).

As the methodology of estimating the HDI has been developed under the auspices of UNDP, using data from various agencies, it is best not to attempt to re-invent the wheel and so we use and quote the relevant UNDP Report (1995) itself in order to avoid a second-hand rendering of that methodology.

> The basis for the selection of critical dimensions, and the indicators that make up the human development index, is identifying basic capabilities that people must have to participate in and contribute to society. These include the ability to be knowledgeable and the ability to have access to the resources needed for a decent standard of living.
>
> The HDI has three components: life expectancy at birth; educational attainment (comprising adult literacy, with two-thirds weight, and a combined primary, secondary and tertiary enrollment [*sic*] ratio, with one-third weight); and income.
>
> The HDI value for each country indicates how far that country has to go to attain certain defined goals: an average life span of 85 years, access to education for all and a decent level of income. The closer a country's HDI is to 1, the less the remaining distance that country has to travel.
>
> The treatment of the income component is rather complex. The HDI adjusts real income (in purchasing power parity, or PPP dollars) for the diminishing utility of higher levels of income to human development. The premise is that people do not need an infinite income for a decent standard of living. So, the HDI defines a threshold for income regarded as adequate for a reasonable standard of living. This threshold is the average global real GDP per capita in PPP dollars in 1992, a little more than $5,000. The HDI treats income up to this level at full value, but income beyond it as having a sharply diminishing utility – for which a specific formula is used.
>
> The HDI reduces all three basic indicators to a common measuring rod by measuring achievement in each indicator as the relative distance from a desirable goal. The maximum and minimum values for each variable are reduced to a scale between 0 and 1, with each country at some point on this scale.
>
> The HDI is constructed by (1) defining a country's measure of relative achievement in each of the three basic variables and (2) taking a simple average of the three indicators.
>
> (The detailed method for constructing the HDI is explained in technical note 3 of the UNDP Report 1995).

The methodology of preparing the HDI goes a long way towards removing many of the limitations which other indicators have and turns out to be the best method used till now for assessing an aggregate level of development for each country and a meaningful comparison with the levels of other countries. The HDI level of a given country measures, as the UNDP Report states, the distance which a country has yet to travel on the path of human development as judged by attainments in income generation, education and expectation of life at birth. The higher the HDI of a country, that is the closer it is to 1, the lesser is the distance that country has to travel towards the ideal level.

However, the HDI itself is not entirely free from blemishes. In the final analysis, the aggregate HDI index ends up in a horizontal summing up of three different levels of development (income, education and longevity) within a country in a unweighted manner, that is, assigning equal importance to each of these three factors – and we know that an unweighted index is an arbitrarily weighted index. How are we to be sure that income, education and longevity stand in an equal weightage of 1:1:1? We are not sure, and hence some arbitrariness seems to be creeping into the HDI methodology.

Moreover, even if income and educational levels are deemed to be independent of each other – and that may not be the case – how do we know that longevity, measured by life expectancy at birth, is an entirely independent factor? Is not longevity affected by income levels and, indeed, by educational levels which provide better awareness and information to the people to adjust their life style, so as to achieve a longer life and longer life expectancy? However, these limitations of the HDI would seem to be relatively minor blemishes compared to those in the other indicators of levels of development.

RESULTS IN TERMS OF HDI

When estimates of human development index are obtained for the 24 countries under our consideration in five different categories, the following appear to be some of the important findings (Table 9.1):

(i) The HDI is at a much higher level, approaching 1, in the developed market economies of Group 1 as compared to any other group of countries;

(ii) For the countries in Groups 1 and 2, that is the developed market economies and planned economies, HDI has generally deteriorated over the period 1985 to 1993. HDI for Group 1, however, shows improvement in 1993 as compared to 1992. This may well be owing to the recovery of these economies from a prolonged recession.

Table 9.1
Human Development Index and Change Over Time

Country	Human development index 1985	1993
1. Developed market economies		
USA	0.980	0.940
Japan	0.997	0.938
Australia	0.982	0.929
Germany	0.959	0.920
UK	0.974	0.924
2. Planned economies		
Hungary	0.932	0.855
Poland	0.936	0.819
Russian Federation	–	0.804
Kazakhstan	–	0.740
Ukraine	–	0.719
3. Developing market economies		
Korea	0.874	0.886
Singapore	0.914	0.881
Malaysia	0.828	0.826
Indonesia	0.531	0.641
Saudi Arabia	0.729	0.772
4. Mixed economies		
Brazil	0.807	0.796
China	0.614	0.609
Pakistan	0.355	0.442
India	0.370	0.436
Kenya	0.432	0.473
5. Least developed economies		
Bangladesh	0.265	0.365
Cambodia	0.175	0.325
Ethiopia	0.166	0.237
Niger	0.158	0.204

Source: *Human Development Report*, UNDP (various issues).

In the case of the planned economies of Group 2, the HDI has generally deteriorated, indicating a fall in the standard of living in the former socialist countries as compared to the levels attained in the past.
(iii) Among the developing market economies of Group 3 and the mixed
   economies of Group 4, whereas HDI is almost 'sticky' for many
   countries, in some countries, such as Saudi Arabia, Indonesia, Pakistan

and India, it has shown a marginal improvement over the eight years 1985–93.

(iv) Though the HDI is steadily rising in the least developed countries of Group 5, it has an extremely low value, which indicates the serious nature of poverty of all forms.

REAL GNP PER CAPITA

In Chapter 5 we gave the levels of per capita income in real terms for all the 24 selected countries in the five categories, as well as the change in these levels, depicting real income growth between 1985 and 1993. For ready reference, we repeat in Table 9.2 the real GNP levels prevailing in these two years. Suffice it to say here that in the latest year (1993), the per capita real income in terms of purchasing power parity dollars was the highest in Group 1 and ranged from US$24 680 for the USA to US$17 230 for the UK. In the planned economies of Group 2, the range was from $6059 (Hungary) to $3250 (Ukraine); the developing market economies of Group 3 ranged from $19 350 (Singapore) to $3270 (Indonesia); the mixed economies from $5550 (Brazil) to $1240 (India); and the least developed economies showed a range from $1290 in the case of Bangladesh to $790 in Niger.

It is also observed that between 1985 and 1993, nearly all the selected economies showed an enhancement in per capita incomes so that average poverty could be said to have diminished. Figures for the ex-Soviet areas are not comparable but from all accounts their per capita real incomes declined between 1985 and 1993 and thereafter. Somewhat unbelievably though marginally, China's real GNP per capita fell between the two years from $2470 to $2330.

LIFE EXPECTANCY

Life expectancy at birth (in years) has generally been improving for all groups of countries, though there are considerable variations across the countries. Table 9.3 shows the life expectancy data for different countries: life expectancy is above 70 years in the industrialized countries of Group 1 and 2 and below 50 years in the least developed economies.

EDUCATIONAL ATTAINMENTS

Educational attainments, as measured by the combined enrolment ratio in relation to age-specific population, are shown in Table 9.4. The rising ratio in almost all cases indicates a steady improvement in opportunities

Table 9.2
Real GNP Per Capita (PPP$)

Country	1985*	1993
1. Developed market economies		
USA	19 850	24 680
Japan	13 650	20 660
Australia	14 530	18 530
Germany	13 388	18 840
UK	13 060	17 230
2. Planned economies		
Hungary	5 920	6 059
Poland	4 190	4 702
Russian Federation		4 760
Kazakhstan	6 270**	3 710
Ukraine		3 250
3. Developing market economies		
Korea	5 680	9 710
Singapore	10 540	19 350
Malaysia	5 070	8 360
Indonesia	1 820	3 270
Saudi Arabia	9 350	12 600
4. Mixed economies		
Brazil	4 620	5 500
China	2 470	2 330
Pakistan	1 790	2 160
India	870	1 240
Kenya	1 010	1 400
5. Least developed economies		
Bangladesh	720	1 290
Cambodia	1 000	1 250
Ethiopia	350	420
Niger	610	790

* Refers to 1985–8.
** USSR. Figures are not comparable owing to changes in methods of esti-
mation and currency values.
Source: *Human Development Report* issues for 1991 and for 1996, UNDP.

for learning and for the general educational and professional development
of the people. Here too, Group 1 countries are considerably ahead of
others, including the planned economies of Group 2. There are wide differences across the groups and within a Group, as may be seen in Table 9.4.
The mixed economies of Group 4 and the least developed economies of
Group 5 are generally much below the levels attained by other groups of
countries.

Table 9.3
Life Expectancy and Change Over Time

Country	Life expectancy	
	1988	*1993*
1. Developed market economies		
USA	76.0	76.1
Japan	78.0	79.6
Australia	76.0	77.8
Germany	75.0	76.1
UK	75.0	76.3
2. Planned economies		
Hungary	70.0	69.0
Poland	72.0	71.1
Russian Federation	–	67.4
Kazakhstan	–	69.7
Ukraine	–	69.3
3. Developing market economies		
Korea	70.0	71.3
Singapore	74.0	79.4
Malaysia	70.0	70.9
Indonesia	61.0	63.0
Saudi Arabia	64.0	69.9
4. Mixed economies		
Brazil	65.0	66.5
China	70.0	66.6
Pakistan	55.0	61.8
India	58.0	60.7
Kenya	59.0	55.5
5. Least developed economies		
Bangladesh	51.0	55.9
Cambodia	–	51.9
Ethiopia	47.0	47.8
Niger	45.0	46.7

Source: *Human Development Report*, UNDP (various issues).

The countries showing a combined enrolment ratio below 50 per cent for the age-specific population are: Pakistan (37%), Bangladesh (40%), Cambodia (30%), Ethiopia (16%) and Niger (15%).

STRONG RELATIONSHIP OF THE THREE COMPONENTS OF HDI WITH THE HDI AND WITH EACH OTHER

Our confidence in the efficacy of the human development index (HDI) – as a measure of the distance covered by a country and the distance yet to

Table 9.4
Educational Attainment and Change Over Time

Country	Educational attainment (combined enrolment ratio)	
	1985	*1993*
1. Developed market economies		
USA	70.1	96.0
Japan	69.5	78.0
Australia	69.1	79.0
Germany	68.9	79.0
UK	69.6	83.0
2. Planned economies		
Hungary	68.9	67.0
Poland	67.8	76.0
Russian Federation	68.5	79.0
Kazakhstan	–	65.0
Ukraine	–	76.0
3. Developing market economies		
Korea	65.3	81.0
Singapore	56.5	68.0
Malaysia	50.7	61.0
Indonesia	48.9	61.0
Saudi Arabia	39.5	55.0
4. Mixed economies		
Brazil	53.4	72.0
China	47.1	57.0
Pakistan	21.2	37.0
India	58.0	60.7
Kenya	44.0	56.0
5. Least developed economies		
Bangladesh	22.1	40.0
Cambodia	19.9	30.0
Ethiopia	33.7	16.0
Niger	14.4	15.0

Source: *Human Development Report*, UNDP (various issues).

be covered on the road to poverty annihilation – is firmly established when we notice that the three components of HDI – real GNP per capita, educational attainments and life expectancy – are not only strongly correlated with the HDI but also strongly correlated with each other. Had these three measures been mutually uncorrelated and also uncorrelated with the HDI, the HDI as an average of the three would have been merely an arithmetical concept or a number divorced from any reality on the ground. But the strong correlations which make the HDI move generally in the same direction as its components and the components mutually in the same direction give the HDI a degree of realism and hence acceptability.

Table 9.5 gives the basic data about the ranking of the 24 selected countries in respect of the three components of the HDI as well as the ranking in terms of the HDI itself and Table 9.6 presents the correlation matrix. It turns out that the rank correlation in the case of the 24 selected countries works out as high as 0.75 between real GNP per capita and educational attainments; 0.94 between GNP per capita and life expectancy; and 0.81 between life expectancy and educational attainment. Similarly, the HDI itself for the 24 countries has a rank correlation coefficient of 0.60 and 0.76,

Table 9.5
Ranking of the Selected Countries

Country	HDI 1993	Real GNP per capita (PPP) $ 1993	Life expectancy 1993	Educational attainment 1993
(1)	(2)	(3)	(4)	(5)
USA	1	1	5	1
Japan	2	2	1	5
Australia	3	5	3	4
Germany	5	4	5	4
UK	4	6	4	2
Hungary	8	10	12	9
Poland	10	13	7	6
Russian Federation	11	12	13	4
Kazakhstan	14	14	10	10
Ukraine	15	16	11	6
Korea	6	8	6	3
Singapore	7	3	2	8
Malaysia	9	9	8	11
Indonesia	16	15	16	11
Saudi Arabia	13	7	8	11
Brazil	12	11	15	7
Kenya	18	19	20	13
China	17	17	14	12
Pakistan	19	18	17	16
India	20	22	18	14
Bangladesh	21	20	19	15
Cambodia	22	21	21	17
Ethiopia	23	24	22	18
Niger	24	23	23	19

Table 9.6
Correlation Matrix

Indicators	HDI	GNP per capita	Educational attainment	Life expectancy
HDI	1.00	0.76	0.18	0.60
GNP per capita	0.76	1.00	0.75	0.94
Educational attainment	0.18	0.75	1.00	0.81
Life expectancy	0.60	0.94	0.81	1.00

respectively, with life expectancy and real GNP per capita. The only weak correlation in the matrix is between the HDI and educational attainments, while other correlation coefficients are quite strong.

10 International Differences in Poverty Levels

Relative international poverty is the extent of difference in the levels of living of various countries and is proposed to be measured in terms of a broad index of purchasing power of people. Such an index is derived by a Purchasing Power Parity (PPP) estimate of GNP per capita, which is worked out by the United Nations for inter-country comparisons.

PPP ESTIMATE OF GNP PER CAPITA

Table 10.1 gives estimates of GNP per capita for different countries for 1994 (Column 4). Columns 2 and 3, on the other hand, provide the indices of GNP per capita, for 1987 and 1994 respectively, computed on the basis of United States GNP per capita taken as 100 for both the years. This reveals the relative position of different countries *vis-à-vis* the US levels of income in 1987 and 1994. The following major conclusions emerge.

1. Almost all the countries in Group 1 have realized an increase in their per capita income levels between 1987 and 1994, as compared to the income levels of the US. The position of the UK has, however, marginally deteriorated.
2. Planned economies in Group 2 have recorded a substantial deterioration in their per capita incomes. For some countries, such as Ukraine and Kazakhstan, the relevant indices have been reduced by more than 50 per cent.
3. All the selected market economies of the developing world in Group 3 have considerably improved their per capita income levels before the sharp downturn of 1997–98. The improvements in the indices, however, indicate wide differences across these countries.
4. The mixed economies of Group 4, show a mixed trend in per capita income. China and India have emerged with improved indices – China impressively and India marginally – whereas the position of Brazil, Pakistan and Kenya has deteriorated.
5. Bangladesh in Group 5, has marginally improved but other countries in this Group, namely Ethiopia and Niger, have recorded a decline in the levels of per capita income, which indicates a worsening of poverty in the LDCs.

The Poverty of Nations

Table 10.1
Relative Poverty: Inter-Country Comparison of
GNP Per Capita in Relation to US

Country	PPP estimates of GNP per capita		
	US$100 1987	Current US$100 1994	1994
(1)	(2)	(3)	(4)
1. Developed market economies			
USA	100.0	100.0	25 880
Japan	74.7	81.7	21 140
Australia	69.9	70.0	18 120
Germany	66.1	75.3	19 480
UK	70.0	60.4	17 970
2. Planned economies			
Hungary	28.9	23.5	6 080
Poland	21.4	21.2	5 480
Russian Federation	30.6	17.8	–
Kazakhstan	24.2	10.9	2 810
Ukraine	20.4	10.1	2 620
3. Developing market economies			
Korea	27.3	39.9	10 330
Singapore	60.2	84.6	21 990
Malaysia	23.5	32.6	8 440
Indonesia	10.0	13.9	3 600
Saudi Arabia	45.7	36.6	9 480
4. Mixed economies			
Brazil	24.2	20.9	5 400
China	5.8	9.7	2 510
Pakistan	8.5	8.2	2 130
India	4.4	4.9	1 280
Kenya	5.7	5.1	1 310
5. Least developed economies			
Bangladesh	4.9	5.1	1 330
Cambodia	–	–	–
Ethiopia	2.0	1.7	430
Niger	3.8	3.0	770

Source: *Human Development Report*, UNDP (various issues).

As poverty-stricken population generally clusters at the bottom range of per capita incomes, it is conceivable that per capita income improves and yet poverty increases. But, as poverty is a 'sticky' phenomenon, it is not easily conceivable, nor probable, that per capita income goes down and yet the poverty situation improves. We can, therefore, take the direction of change in per capita income as approximating to the change in poverty levels. Thus, overall, it emerges that relative poverty as compared to US level of income between 1987 and 1994 has deteriorated in the planned economies and in most of the developing countries in Group 4 and Group 5, as may be observed in the Table 10.1.

DISPARITY IN INCOME AND CONSUMPTION

Table 10.2 demonstrates the pattern of distribution of income or consumption among different income groups across the various countries. The following observations may be made.

- The income share of the lowest 20 per cent of income groups is generally higher for the planned economies of Group 2, as compared to the developed market economies of Group 1. Likewise, the income share of the top 20 per cent of income group is lower for Group 2 as compared to Group 1. This indicates a narrower range of disparity in the planned economies as compared to the advanced market economies and a particular concern in Group 2 for better income distribution. These results are corroborated by the Gini index as well.
- Per capita income disparity in Group 3 and 4, as also in Group 5 differs widely across the countries and indicates a mixed behaviour. For example, in Brazil and Kenya the disparity is glaringly high, as indicated by the Gini index, whereas it is less for Bangladesh, Pakistan and Indonesia.

The overall results pertaining to income disparity show a mixed trend for the developed and developing countries and indicate for most countries an adverse situation and hence a concentration of poverty in the lower income brackets.

Table 10.2

Relative Poverty: Distribution of Income or Consumption

Country	Survey year	Gini index	Percentage share of income or consumption						
			Lowest 10%	Lowest 20%	Second quintile	Third quintile	Fourth quintile	Highest 20%	Highest 10%
(1)	(2)	(3)	(4)	(5)	(6)	(7)	(8)	(9)	(10)
1. Developed market economies									
USA	1985	–	–	4.7	11.0	17.4	25.0	41.9	25.0
Japan	1979	–	–	8.7	13.2	17.5	23.1	37.5	22.4
Australia	1985	–	–	4.4	11.1	17.5	24.8	42.2	25.8
Germany	1988	–	–	7.0	11.8	17.1	23.9	40.3	24.4
UK	1988	–	–	4.6	10.0	16.8	24.3	44.3	27.8
2. Planned economies									
Hungary	1993	27.0	4.0	9.5	14.0	17.6	22.3	36.6	22.6
Poland	1992	27.2	4.0	9.3	13.8	17.7	22.6	36.6	22.1
Russian Federation	1993	49.6	1.2	3.7	8.5	13.5	20.4	53.8	38.7
Kazakhstan	1993	32.7	3.1	7.5	12.3	16.9	22.9	40.4	24.9
Ukraine	1992	25.7	4.1	9.5	14.1	18.1	22.9	35.4	20.8
3. Developing market economies									
Korea	–	–	–	–	–	–	–	–	–
Singapore	1983	–	–	5.1	9.9	14.6	21.4	48.4	33.5
Malaysia	1989	48.4	1.9	4.6	8.3	13.0	20.4	53.7	37.9
Indonesia	1993	31.7	3.9	8.7	12.3	16.3	22.1	40.7	25.6
Saudi Arabia	–	–	–	–	–	–	–	–	–

4. Mixed economies

Brazil	1989	63.4	0.7	2.1	4.9	8.9	16.8	67.5	51.3
China	1992	37.6	2.6	6.2	10.5	15.8	23.6	43.9	26.8
Pakistan	1991	31.2	3.4	8.4	12.9	16.9	22.2	39.7	25.2
India	1992	33.8	3.7	8.5	12.1	15.8	21.1	42.6	28.4
Kenya	1992	57.5	1.2	3.4	6.7	10.7	17.0	62.1	47.7

5. Least developed economies

Bangladesh	1992	28.3	4.1	9.4	13.5	17.2	22.0	37.0	23.7
Cambodia	–	–	–	–	–	–	–	–	–
Ethiopia	–	–	–	–	–	–	–	–	–
Niger	1992	36.1	3.0	7.5	11.8	15.5	21.1	44.1	29.3

Source: World Development Report, 1995, The World Bank.

11 Poverty in the Highly Developed Market Economies

The major countries of the North American continent, namely the USA and Canada, and the countries of Western Europe had virtually conquered the problem of poverty in the second half of the nineteenth and the first half of the twentieth century, though the conquest was not total. The advent of the market economy and the phenomena of the great economic revolutions of the eighteenth, nineteenth and twentieth centuries were responsible for lifting up the economic levels of these areas and reducing the extent as well as the intensity of poverty. The revolutions that emerged and coexisted in a telescopic manner comprised urbanization, the agricultural transformation, the commercial and industrial revolutions and, more recently, the technological and communications revolutions. The progress of rationality in the nineteenth century, the shift from autocratic to democratic regimes, the social revolution comprised by the emergence and strengthening of trade unionism, the extension of voting rights ending in adult franchise, the movement to establish the rights of women and the evolution of the welfare state, all played their role in promoting economic growth and social development. These far-reaching occurrences raised the standards and levels of living, created a new dynamism in economic, social and political organization and consolidated the welfare state of the twentieth century with its network of social services focusing, in particular, on education, health, unemployment compensations and old age benefits.

These great processes, on the one hand, were a major cause of economic growth and development and, on the other, raised the masses from the squalor and abject poverty of an earlier era into a decent level of living for nearly everybody. In many important senses, poverty could be said to have been virtually conquered. Many of the aforementioned movements were extended from North America and Western Europe to the newly industrializing areas of Australia, New Zealand and Japan. It was, perhaps, the first time in history that the whole mass of the population in these countries had been subjected to economic and social uplift and it is not an exaggeration to epitomize these developments as major achievements in poverty elimination.

It was no accident that all these economies were industrialized economies with market orientation. The trends of improvement continued in the second half of the twentieth century and these economies were able to overcome the impact of two long-lasting bloody wars in the first half of that century and continue their progress in economic development, social uplift and poverty reduction.

However, even as the advance of the laissez-faire economy brought market freedoms and substantial economic and social benefits, the market economies became subjected to violent economic fluctuations owing to the phenomenon of the trade cycle, in particular, in the late nineteenth and the first half of the twentieth century. The rise and fall of the national product, the increase and decrease in investment activity and the ups and downs of employment and unemployment had the effect of periodic fluctuations in poverty levels. Even as the trend in the growth of these countries tended to reduce poverty, the cyclical fluctuations during the economic downturns and upturns, depressions and recoveries, followed by another and yet another similar cyclical movement, threw masses of people again and again into the category of poverty.

In the second half of the twentieth century, though there were no serious *depressions* of high intensity such as the Great Depression of 1929–33, there have been economic *recessions* of considerable extent and depth, with some differences of definition existing between the two. It can be observed through statistical analyses that in the post World War II era, recessions have been coming with increasing frequency and that each recession has lasted longer than the previous one. Immediately after 1951, recessions only lasted about two years but their duration got extended later on to three to four and even to five years. The recession beginning in 1979 in the USA gripped the rest of the industrial world in 1980 and lasted four years, ending in the USA in 1983 and Western Europe in 1984. But the recession which started around 1991 went on in many industrialized nations till 1996, lasting rather longer than its earlier counterpart.

Between any two recessions, there have been short periods of recovery but these recoveries have been generally quite weak. A recovery has hardly lasted more than a few years when yet another downturn has taken over and soon converted itself into a recession. During the depressions earlier and the recessions more recently, as the national income declines, government's tax revenues go down, huge budget deficits emerge and unemployment takes an ugly turn, throwing large numbers of people out of jobs and economic activity. Unemployment rates in the industrialized nations during recessions have varied from 5 to 10, or even 12 per cent of the workforce, amounting to absolute numbers like four million in Germany and eight million in the USA. The persistence and recurrence of poverty, tempered no doubt by unemployment compensations and other benefits, is writ large in these figures.

Until the mid-1980s, Europe, the United States, Japan and Australia had witnessed an unusual phenomenon, of recession and inflation existing together, and this coexistence of strange bed-fellows came to be called 'stagflation'. The masses of the poorer population in these countries suffered on the one hand through unemployment and, on the other, through inflation. By this time the industrialized states had evolved various methods of providing economic cushions, including public services, social safety nets (particularly in terms of unemployment benefits), retirement benefits, maternity benefits and old age payments in different degrees – more so in Western Europe and less so, perhaps, in the USA. Medical services, health benefits and other cushions had also been provided and all this reduced somewhat the serious impact of emerging poverty – emerging basically through unemployment. But as the revenues of the governments also decline seriously during recessions, these social services are subjected to great strain and this causes a fear of reduction – if they are not actually reduced. In the public mind the fear of unemployment is as potent a factor as the fear of inflation. The shortage of revenue and the need for larger social services during the recessions forces the industrialized state into huge borrowing, both at home and abroad, and raises the problem of mounting national debt and its servicing.

Meanwhile, it is worth noting that between 60 and 70 per cent of the exports of the countries in the first world are to other countries within the first world. But during recessionary times, these intra-first world exports decline to a figure between 50 and 60 per cent of their total exports. As the recessionary phenomena are basically prevalent within the first world – the extraordinary collapse of the South-East Asian economies being an exception – the failure to export to the richest part of the world causes a depression in the export industries and brings about further unemployment in the first world economies. It is clear that unemployment is the basic cause of poverty escalation from time to time in the first world and brings with it a series of other deprivations and miseries at the social level. Some of these miseries are, perhaps, independent of the recessions and unemployment, but others are linked to these occurrences. Alongside unemployment, Western societies appear to be subjected to other social and economic problems such as high divorce rates – which negatively impact the younger generation – the emergence of new diseases while the old ones are conquered, the problem of drugs and drunkenness and of extremist and terrorist activities. The last-named phenomenon is known to have strong links with unemployment and economic degradation of societies and has raised its ugly head both in Western and Eastern societies. If recessions in the industrial world are the basic malaise which causes unemployment and allied phenomena (which, in turn, lead to a resurgence of poverty), it is important to diagnose the causes of these recessions in the industrial world so that policy action is launched and focused on the reduction or elimination of these causes of poverty.

This exercise of identifying the root causes of recessions has been going on for several decades and many alternative causalities have been diagnosed. The exercise is not yet complete and a recognized and agreed body of thought on which most analysts could converge is not yet in sight. But it seems that a few crucial factors can be held responsible for this phenomenon.

A characteristic feature of Western society is a high rate of saving and the accumulation of capital stock. This capital stock, reduced at the margin through depreciation and obsolescence but increasing as a result of renewal, replacement and expansion, is informed by newer technologies in each successive period of time. Technology has to do, among other things, with the quality of capital stock and consumer goods and services and it is obvious that in the industrialized world, an increasing capital stock goes hand in hand with improved technologies. The market economy which is the hallmark of the Western world today promotes competitiveness and profit augmentation and thereby innovation and inventiveness (in order to withstand competition from other innovative and inventive sources). This competitiveness further enhances the quality as well as the quantity of capital stock. At the end of the day one finds that the great abundance of high-quality capital stock has a tendency, through its very abundance, to lower the rate of return to itself. With a lower rate of return to new capital projects, fresh investment in these projects slows down, as capital build-up is a function of the rate of return to capital. Thus, even as newer technology tends to enhance the rate of return to capital, the consequent abundance of capital stock in a highly competitive situation causes a decline in the rate of return and slows down the rate of increase of capital.

At the same time, Western industrialized societies have been experiencing yet another phenomenon associated with capital stock. Where large amounts of this stock are available, and by implication large amounts of consumer goods, including durable consumer goods, there is likely to be a saturation of demand and then a reduction in new demand. To give a simple illustration, when a family has one car there may be a strong case to have a second one; but when each of, say, four members of a family have a car, the case for a fifth car is not established. And that is true of numerous other items such as refrigerators, air-conditioners, computers, telephones, fax machines, foods, clothing and so on. Thus, in Western societies, where there is a great abundance of goods and services which can be accessed by even the lowermost income rungs of society, incremental demand at the margin has begun to decline. As the profitability of capital goods, among other things, emanates from the profitability of consumer goods, and durable consumer goods at that, and as the demand for these is not expanding as before, the capital goods industry begins to show declining profitability. This is why the entrepreneurs in Western economies do not have on their shelves as many projects as they used to have in relation to the GNP. That is how a 6 per cent growth of the US economy, a 5 per cent growth of the European economies and a 12 per cent growth of the Japanese economy, over sustained periods in the early 1960s, has given way to a much smaller and declining growth rate of these economies – say 2 per cent during recovery and 0.5 per cent during recessions – in the1970s, 1980s and 1990s.

Table 11.1 gives the annual five-yearly average growth rate of GDP at constant prices in the leading industrial economies of the USA, France, FRG, UK and Japan. It will be seen from this table that as a rule the quinquennial average of annual growth rates has been declining consistently in all these economies. The USA's five-yearly average of growth rate has come down from 4.68 per cent during the 1961–5 period to 3.02 per cent during 1966–70, to 2.64 per cent during 1986–90 and to 2.33 per cent during 1991–4. Similarly, France moved downwards from a 5.86 per cent growth rate during the early 1960s to a 3.22 per cent rate in the late 1980s and to less than 1 per cent in the early 1990s. Growth rate in West

Table 11.1
Growth Rate of GDP at Constant Prices
Selected Industrial Economies

5-Year period (1)	USA (2)	France (3)	Germany (4)	UK (5)	Japan (6)	India (7)
1961–65	4.68	5.86	4.86	3.20	12.48	2.96
1966–70	3.02	5.38	4.20	2.50	11.00	4.86
1971–75	2.44	4.02	2.20	2.20	4.40	3.02
1976–80	3.30	3.54	3.36	1.72	4.98	3.60
1981–85	2.56	1.50	1.28	1.88	3.96	5.24
1986–90	2.64	3.22	3.26	3.34	4.54	6.38
1991–94	2.33	0.83	1.03	0.09	1.60	2.87

Source: *International Financial Statistics – Year Book.*

Germany also dwindled down from 4.86 per cent in the early 1960s to 3.26 per cent in the late 1990s and 1.03 per cent in the early 1990s. The growth rate of the United States admittedly rose from 2.2 per cent in the early 1960s to 3.34 per cent, but it then collapsed to 0.9 per cent in the last quinquennium. Japan, the shining example of high and rising growth rates in the 1960s, had its growth chopped from an impressive 12.48 per cent in the early 1960s to 4.54 per cent in the late 1980s and to only 1.60 per cent in the early 1990s.

As distinct from the five-yearly average, Table 11.2 gives the annual GDP growth at constant prices between 1984 and 1995 and underlines the same characteristic of a collapsed and frustrated growth, hovering between 4 per cent and 1 per cent in all these five leading economies. Ever since the early 1980s, it appears, the GDP growth rates have moved away from the higher growth path of an earlier era and are lingering on at substantially lower figures, except in the USA.

As argued earlier, one of the basic causes of declining growth rates of GNP or GDP can be found in declining investment rates in the advanced economies. A trend decline of growth rates over several decades can itself be a cause of a declining trend in investment rates. But, apart from this and a few other causes, the lower rate of return to capital and the declining consumer demand at the margin seem to be strong factors behind a decline in investment rates.

Table 11.2
Annual Growth of GDP at Constant Prices (1984–95)

Year (1)	USA (2)	France (3)	Germany* (4)	UK (5)	Japan (6)
1984	6.2	1.3	2.8	2.3	4.5
1985	3.2	1.9	1.9	3.8	5.0
1986	2.9	2.5	2.2	4.3	2.6
1987	3.1	2.3	1.5	4.8	4.3
1988	3.9	4.5	3.7	5.0	6.2
1989	2.5	4.3	4.0	2.2	4.8
1990	0.8	2.5	4.9	0.4	4.8
1991	2.6	3.2	3.6	3.3	4.5
1992	−1.2	1.3	1.2	−0.5	1.4
1993	3.3	−1.5	−2.3	2.3	0.1
1994	4.1	2.7	1.6	3.8	0.6
1995	2.3	0.8	1.0	0.9	1.6

*Includes East Germany from 1991.
Source: *Economic and Social Survey 1995*, The World Bank.

Table 11.3 gives the actual five-yearly average of investment as a per cent of GDP in the five leading industrial economies. Here too it becomes clear that, in general, the investment percentage to GDP has either been declining slowly or is more or less constant. France, Germany and Japan are clear cases of a decline in investment and, perhaps, the UK too, though the USA – the most resilient of the industrial economies which emerged from the latest recession rather early and has been showing a strong recovery in the middle of 1990s – exhibits a constant investment to GDP ratio.

In respect of annual data, the investment-GDP percentage from 1980 to 1993 is seen in Table 11.4. And here too, there is no evidence of any increase in investment rate but rather of a mild decline despite a general increase over the years in per capita incomes. It will also be seen that the GDP growth rates and investment rates take a downward direction during the recessionary periods and rise during the recovery phases.

As one might expect, during recessionary periods unemployment rises disturbingly high and employment declines to lower levels. But recessions apart, the trend rate of unemployment has been upwards during the 1970s and the 1980s. As Table 11.5 depicting the percentage of labour force unemployed from 1970 to 1985 shows, unemployment in the USA moved from 5 per cent, via 8 and 9 per cent to 7.1 per cent. France shows a growth of unemployment from 4 per cent in the mid-1970s to 10 per cent in the mid-1980s; Germany (FRG) from less than 1 per cent in the early 1970s to around 9 per cent in the mid-1980s; the UK from around 3.5 per cent in the early 1970s to 11 per cent in the mid-1980s and Japan from 1.2 per cent in the early 1970s to 2.6 per cent in the mid-1980s.

Table 11.3
**Annual Five-Yearly Average Investment as
Percentage of GDP**

5-Year period	USA	France	Germany	UK	Japan
(1)	(2)	(3)	(4)	(5)	(6)
1961–65	18.8	24.1	27.5	18.5	30.1
1966–70	23.0	25.7	25.5	19.8	36.3
1971–75	18.9	25.3	24.0	20.1	35.9
1976–80	19.7	24.0	22.1	19.2	31.7
1981–85	18.2	20.3	20.3	16.4	29.3
1986–90	18.4	21.2	20.1	19.1	30.3
1991–93	15.8	19.5	20.6	15.3	31.4

Source: *International Financial Statistics – Year Book.*

Table 11.4
Investment as Percentage of GDP

Years (1)	USA (2)	France (3)	Germany (4)	UK (5)	Japan (6)
1980	20.0	24.2	23.2	16.8	32.2
1981	20.9	21.7	20.8	15.1	31.1
1982	18.4	21.9	19.3	15.6	29.9
1983	18.4	19.9	20.2	16.4	28.1
1984	21.2	19.0	20.2	17.3	28.0
1985	20.1	18.9	19.5	17.2	28.2
1986	19.4	19.6	19.4	17.1	27.8
1987	18.9	20.2	19.2	18.0	28.6
1988	18.4	21.4	19.9	20.3	30.6
1989	18.2	22.3	20.7	21.0	31.8
1990	16.9	22.5	21.2	19.2	32.8
1991	18.4	21.2	20.1	19.1	30.3
1992	15.7	19.7	21.0	15.2	31.2
1993	15.8	19.5	20.6	15.3	31.4

Source: *International Financial Statistics – Year Book* 1994 UN (various issues) IMF.

Table 11.5, focusing on the period 1980–85, shows a continuation of a high rate of unemployment in all the major industrial economies. The figures of unemployment percentage are no longer in the range of 2, 3 and 4 per cent – except for Japan – but stay in the 5–10 per cent zone, or even above, for all these countries. The USA has constantly shown an unemployment rate of between 5 and 7 per cent resulting in an absolute number of 8.7 million unemployed in 1993. France shows disastrous unemployment rates, seldom less than 9 per cent of the labour force and going up to 12.5 per cent in 1994. Germany, which with Japan, performed the miracle of economic recovery in the 1950s, languishes with an unemployment rate which is never less than 6 per cent and goes up to 9 per cent at the worst times – and the latter percentage means an absolute unemployment of about four million workers. The United Kingdom has also fallen into the unemployment trap by even bigger margins, its unemployment percentage in relation to labour force ranging between 6.8 per cent at the best of times to 11.2 per cent at the worst – a serious scar on the face of the UK economy. Of all the industrialized nations studied here, Japan alone has managed to maintain a low unemployment rate since 1984, ranging between 2 per cent and 3 per cent irrespective of recessions and recoveries.

Table 11.5
Percentage of Labour Force Unemployed

Years (1)	USA (2)	France (3)	Germany (4)	UK (5)	Japan (6)
1970	4.9	–	0.7	2.6	1.2
1971	5.9	–	0.8	3.5	1.2
1972	5.6	–	1.1	3.8	1.4
1973	4.9	–	1.2	2.7	1.3
1974	5.6	–	2.6	2.6	1.4
1975	8.5	4.1	4.7	4.1	1.9
1976	7.7	–	4.6	5.7	2.0
1977	7.1	4.7	4.5	6.2	2.0
1978	6.1	5.2	4.3	6.1	2.0
1979	5.8	5.9	3.8	5.7	2.1
1980	7.1	6.3	3.8	7.3	2.0
1981	7.6	7.3	5.5	11.1	2.2
1982	9.7	8.0	7.5	13.1	2.4
1983	9.6	8.0	9.1	13.1	2.7
1984	7.4	9.8	8.7	11.2	2.7
1985	7.1	10.2	9.3	11.2	2.6
1986	6.9	10.4	8.8	11.2	2.8
1987	6.1	10.5	9.0	10.7	2.8
1988	5.4	10.0	8.7	8.8	2.5
1989	5.2	9.4	8.0	7.2	2.3
1990	5.4	8.9	7.0	6.8	2.1
1991	6.6	9.4	6.0	8.3	2.1
1992	7.3	10.4	–	9.6	2.2
1993	6.7	11.6	6.1	10.3	2.5
1994	6.0	12.5	6.9	9.5	2.9
1995	5.8	12.3	6.3	8.3	2.8

Source: *UN Statistical Year Book* (various issues) and World Economic & Social Survey 1995.

The declining growth rates of GNP, the languishing and sluggish rates of investment and the exorbitant and perhaps growing rates of unemployment in the Western economies suggest that the conquest of poverty achieved earlier in the twentieth century is turning into defeat. Newer dimensions of poverty and perhaps newer forms have been emerging in these industrialized market economies. The high levels of economic performance, the large capital stock and state-of-the-art technologies, may cover up the fact of emerging poverty, confined as it is to pockets of unemployment. What also obscures poverty is the capability built up in these economies to provide comprehensive social services and unemployment benefits which cushion the impact of emerging poverty – and this is what matters crucially.

Perhaps the immediate as well as the long-term solutions to the problem of recurring recessions are to be found in

(i) nuclear and non-nuclear disarmament, turning the resources saved into peace dividends for gains in the civilian economy;

(ii) augmentation of trade with other areas of the world in Asia, Latin America and Africa and generating employment in the production and the foreign trade sectors.

This latter approach by the advanced countries, to save themselves from poverty, and the necessary conditions required to implement this method, are matters which require the resolution of many a thorny issue but which also have a vast potential for the conquest of the remaining poverty in the industrialized and highly developing economies.

12 Poverty in India

INTRODUCTION

As one-sixth of the world's population lives in India and a large percentage of it is poor, its uplift from poverty is of crucial importance to the world as well as to India, for, as the dictum has it, 'Poverty anywhere is a danger to prosperity everywhere'.

This chapter deals with *absolute* poverty and *percentage* poverty in India at different points of time. That is to say, it deals with the absolute number and proportion of people who, on different criteria of poverty, could be classified as poor and non-poor in given years. To be sure, it does not deal with relative poverty, that is, with how poor the poor are relative to the rich; it does not deal with income distribution.

All poverty lines are arbitrary and change with time and space, not to mention individual 'inner feelings'. As Peter Cutler (1984) has pointed out,

> Poverty can be defined as more than just a set of physical requirements for physical efficiency. It may also be defined with reference to the norms for society, and conceived as a set of "basic needs" rather than minimum needs. Basic needs would include those material comforts that give people an element of choice. Obviously, such material basic needs will depend upon the culture of the society in question and upon the general standard of living.... There are many layers of "perceived poverty" and they change for individuals and groups over time.
>
> Even so, when we are defining poverty, it is reasonable to take into account widespread norms of consumption whose absence would be a cause for scorn or pity among more affluent groups of people.

This book also conceives of poverty lines, not as minimum calories or even income to keep body and soul together, but as basic needs including some material comforts which are widely perceived by Indian society as necessary and in which people have some choice.

Whatever may be the findings of this work in respect of trends in poverty, the absolute mass as well as the percentage of the poor in India is so staggering that nothing that is stated here can be interpreted as an argument for a reduction or a let-up in the public and private effort towards poverty annihilation. In fact, that effort has to be redoubled.

UNSATISFACTORY POVERTY ESTIMATES WHICH EXCLUDE NON-FOOD ITEMS AND PUBLIC GOODS

Scholars and analysts of the Indian scene have generally come to the conclusion that between 1951 and today the number of people below the poverty line has increased massively and that the proportion of the poor in the total population has remained approximately constant. On close examination, this does not appear to be the case and there is overwhelming evidence to show that the incidence of poverty has been declining, in more senses than one.

It has become fashionable to divide the population on the basis of the National Sample Survey (NSS) data between those who consume less and those who consume more than 2400 calories (rural) or 2100 calories (urban), and then designate the former poor and the latter non-poor. In alternative formulations where instead of calories a minimum family income or expenditure level, say Rs 6300 per annum, is taken as a norm, that income or expenditure is so chosen as to accommodate the minimum calorie requirements. This normative income or expenditure is designated 'the poverty line' and the population above this is regarded as non-poor and that below it is considered to be poor. On such a reckoning, the poverty proportion (the proportion of the poor to total population) in India is seen to have stagnated over the years between 1951 and 1981 at around 52 to 48 per cent.

The 1983–4 round of the National Sample Survey (NSS), however, has shown that even on an expenditure-based or calorie-based reckoning, the poverty proportion has for the first time come down to 37 per cent even though, owing to rapid population growth, the numbers of the non-poor as well as the poor have increased. Nevertheless, the rate of increase of the non-poor turns out to be higher than that of the poor.

The first serious objection to the use of such indices of poverty, based entirely on calorie values or on personal expenditures linked with calorie values, is that these indices are one-sided, partial and biased in the direction of exaggerating the poverty situation. When people's income increases, their food consumption does not increase proportionately as the income elasticity of demand for food has always been less than 1, even for the poor. People are bound rather rigidly by traditional food habits and do not change these very much even when they become prosperous. People do not seem to be getting out of food poverty very easily or very quickly and food poverty lingers on rather longer than other forms of poverty. Indices of poverty based on calories or food consumption thus have a built-in depressor within themselves and fail to note the varied improvements in the non-food realm of poverty.

The second objection is that there are several other, perhaps equally important, forms of poverty such as the poverty of literacy, of education, of health, of housing and of industrial consumer goods, which the calorie-based and food-based indices totally leave out of reckoning; and it is here that major improvements have been emerging. It turns out that people try to get out of these other poverties rather faster than they annihilate food poverty. By concentrating on an index of poverty which people discard later rather than sooner, many economists and policy analysts seem to be reaching unwarranted conclusions about the 'stickiness' of Indian poverty.

The third and perhaps the most critical objection is that people in India purchase their food and many other necessities through their own expenditures but typically do not purchase their literacy, their education and their health goods in this manner. The rich in urban areas do send their children to public schools and elite colleges and are patients in paid hospitals and clinics. But these are relatively few. Millions of students in schools and colleges and millions of patients in hospitals, primary health centres and sub-centres do not pay wholly for their literacy, education and health services. These are either heavily subsidized or supplied entirely at the state's expense; and personal expenditure data do not capture all this massive consumption which is met from State services. Personal expenditure data thus grossly understate the reduction of poverty through public goods.

An alternative approach, then, is to focus on different aspects of poverty, including of course nutritional poverty, but also including those other important forms of poverty such as illiteracy, lack of education and absence of access to health-care services which people at this period in India seem to be at least as keen to overcome as they are to overcome nutritional poverty. This approach enables us, however imperfectly, to get out of the straitjacket of personal expenditure data and consider the poverty situation as it is emerging through the availability of public goods and services. As several scholars have examined the calorie-based poverty in India and have used the personal expenditure approach, this book pays attention to the public goods aspect.

HYPOTHESES ABOUT POVERTY REDUCTION

Poverty elimination is a slow process especially in countries with a history of colonial domination and laissez-faire governments. It appears from India's case that to establish a link between the growth of the national product and the various aspects of poverty reduction, a series of hypotheses can be set up and examined. These hypotheses – which may well depict the general behaviour in many densely populated developing countries – suggest that if colonial domination ends, popular governments responsive to public opinion emerge, and all goes well with the process of planned development, the elimination of poverty proceeds through three phases – though things become worse before they become better.

Phase 1

The first phase before (and even after) independence represents the initial conditions whose main characteristics are as follows:

1A

1. The national product declines or increases very slowly.
2. Population keeps growing – but not too fast, as death rates are high – and keeps cutting into the national product.
3. Per capita income declines.

(In India's case, between 1901 and 1951, the national product grew at a slow trend rate of 1 per cent per year; population increased at 1.25 per cent per year; and per capita product declined approximately by about 0.25 per cent per year.)

1B

4. Taking one aspect of poverty such as illiteracy (we could as well take lack of education, ill health or malnutrition), the percentage of illiterates may increase (or decrease imperceptibly) as the facilities for literacy do not grow proportionately to population and the new population is progressively illiterate.
5. The percentage of literates may decrease (or increase very marginally).

1C

6. The absolute number of illiterates grows.
7. The absolute number of literates may increase at best, or may even decrease.

Phase 2

With the coming of national independence, as the state's anti-poverty programmes take over and resources are consciously devoted to investment for economic growth, some basic changes occur in the second phase. The key features of this phase seem to be as follows:

2A

8. The national product increases at a higher trend rate (3.5 per cent per year for 25 years in India's case).
9. Population grows at a faster rate than before (2.4 per cent per year in India), as death rates decline, thanks to more extensive health measures, medical services and public consciousness.
10. Per capita income begins to increase slowly (about 1 per cent per year in India in this phase).

2B

11. Focusing again on some specific dimensions of poverty, the percentage of illiterates, uneducated and unhealthy population begins to decrease.
12. The percentage of literate, educated and healthy population increases.

2C

13. The absolute number of illiterate, uneducated and unhealthy people continues to grow (even though the percentages are declining) as population growth is quite rapid.
14. The absolute number of literate, educated and healthy population also increases.

Phase 3

In the third phase, some structural changes emerge. Agriculture with greater irrigation cushions against starvation and new technologies begins to exhibit 'green revolutionary' trends. Price controls are reduced, imports and industrial licences are liberalized, import-substituting industries become more competitive and some technological changes become evident. Growth strategies and anti-poverty efforts begin to tell and growth rates are increased. The main features in this phase are as shown below:

3A

15. Growth rate of the national product is raised (to about 5 per cent per year, since 1975, in India's case).

16. While death rates continue to decline, with further extension and improvement in medical and health services, and in public consciousness, the birth rate begins to decline as family planning is progressively adopted; and population growth slows down somewhat (to 2 per cent per year in India).
17. Per capita income begins to rise at a faster annual rate (3 per cent in India) and some 'trickle-down' effects of economic growth, absent in earlier phases, now begin to emerge.

3B

18. Along with better access to literacy, education, nutrition, health and industrial consumer goods, the percentage of illiterate, uneducated and unhealthy population declines rather faster.
19. The percentage of literate, educated and healthy people increases at a higher rate.

3C

20. The absolute number of illiterate, uneducated and unhealthy population begins to decline.
21. The absolute number of literate, educated and healthy population increases rapidly and these categories begin to exceed the illiterates, the uneducated and the unhealthy. Even more importantly, the younger population becomes predominantly literate, educated and presumably healthier.

In what follows, we proceed to test some of these hypotheses and examine the changes in some important aspects of poverty in India, especially those that have to do with the consumption of or access to public goods and services like literacy, education and health. Owing to paucity of data for phase 1, this work has to focus on phase 2 and phase 3, together spanning the period 1951 to 1991 – and in some aspects up to 1995.

POVERTY ESTIMATES BASED ON CONSUMPTION EXPENDITURES

Poverty in India is traditionally measured on the basis of consumption-expenditure data periodically gathered by the National Sample Survey Organization (NSSO). The relevant data describe the socio-economic well-being of people and go beyond the confines of minimum nutritional requirements. In essence, poverty estimates based on consumption expenditure reflect purchasing power (i.e. the capacity to satisfy minimum needs of food and non-food items). There are, however, differences in the estimates of the poor, as worked out by the Planning Commission on the one hand and the Expert Group on the other. These differences are due to conceptual and statistical factors as well as technical methodology estimating the number of poor in the country at different points of time. While the methodological aspects will probably remain debatable, the results of various exercises conclusively indicate that the incidence of poverty is declining, though a large number of people continue to suffer from serious levels of material deprivation.

Table 12.1, which is based on the estimates produced by the Planning Commission, demonstrates that the poverty ratio (i.e. the percentage of people below the defined poverty line) has declined from 37.4 per cent in 1983–4 to 18.9 per cent in 1993–4, a decline of 18.5 per cent points in 10 years. The corresponding reduction in the number of poor was 168.2 m in 1993–4, as compared to 271 m in 1983–4 – a reduction of 102.8 m in a decade. The relevant break down for rural and urban areas may be seen in the table.

Another estimate of poverty made by the Expert Group confirms the declining trend in the incidence of poverty but shows that the extent of alleviation in poverty is not as large as indicated in the Planning Commission's estimates. Table 12.2 represents the comparative picture and shows that the poverty ratio has declined from 44.8 per cent in 1983–4 to 39 per cent in 1993–4 – a decline of 5.8 per cent points only. Obviously, the number of the poor emerging from this estimate is still as high as 345 m. Thus, over the period 1983–93, whereas the Planning Commission's estimate shows a reduction in the number of poor by 102.8 m, the Expert Group's estimate shows an increase in the number by about 19 m. However, relative poverty is seen to have declined whether one uses the Planning Commission's reckoning or the Expert Group's estimates.

POVERTY OF LITERACY

It emerges from successive censuses of population that the Indian population grew, as seen in Column 2 of Table 12.3, from 361 m in 1951 to 846 m in 1991, and that the number of literates increased, as seen in Column 4, from 56 m to 384 m in those years.

In India, children below the age of five years, for whom the question of literacy or illiteracy is irrelevant, are quite numerous. Taking the difference

Table 12.1
Number and Percentage of Persons Below Poverty Line in India

| Period | Poverty line (in rupees) | | Poverty ratio (in per cent) | | | No. of the poor (in millions) | | |
| | Rural | Urban | Rural | Urban | Combined | Rural | Urban | Combined |
(1)	(2)	(3)	(4)	(5)	(6)	(7)	(8)	(9)
1983	101.80	117.5	40.40	28.10	37.40	221.50	49.50	271.00
1987–8	131.80	152.1	33.40	20.10	29.90	196.00	41.70	237.70
1988–9	142.50	164.2	22.50	14.20	20.40	136.60	29.10	165.50
1989–90	152.50	170.1	20.30	13.30	18.50	125.20	28.00	153.20
1990–1	169.60	195.0	19.70	10.80	17.40	123.60	23.40	147.00
1991 July–Dec	191.20	220.7	20.50	12.90	18.50	130.30	29.00	159.30
1992 Jan–Dec	210.40	242.8	22.90	13.00	20.30	147.60	29.50	177.20
1993–4*	–		21.70	11.60	18.90	141.10	27.10	168.20

Source: Planning Commission Reproduced in India: *Economic Reforms and Growth* by IMF, 1995. The poverty estimates up to 1987–8 are based on the quinquennial national sample survey whereas the poverty estimates for 1988–9 to1992 are of about one-fifth of the detailed quinquennial surveys. The results of these 'thin samples' must therefore be interpreted with caution when assessing trends in poverty over time.
*obtained from 'Indian's Social Sectors', *CMIE*, 1996, Table 272, p. 261.

Table 12.2
Incidence of Poverty

	1983–4		1987–8		1993–4	
	Expert Group (1)	*Planning Commission* (2)	*Expert Group* (3)	*Planning Commission* (4)	*Expert Group* (5)	*Planning Commission* (6)
Rural (m)	251.7	221.5	229.4	196.0	261.2	141.0
(%)	(45.6)	(40.4)	(39.1)	(33.4)	(40.2)	(21.7)
Urban (m)	75.3	49.5	83.4	41.7	84.6	27.1
(%)	(42.2)	(28.1)	(40.1)	(20.1)	(36.2)	(11.6)
Total (m)	327.0	271.0	312.8	237.7	345.8	168.2
(%)	(44.8)	(37.4)	(39.3)	(29.9)	(39.0)	(18.9)

Source: Compiled from *India's Social Sectors*. CMIE, Bombay p. 261.

Table 12.3
**Numbers and Proportions of Literates
and Illiterates**

Year (1)	Population (m) (2)	Population of age 5 years and above (m) (3)	Number of literates (m) (4)	Number of illiterates (Col. 3–4) (m) (5)	Literacy rate per cent (Col. $4/3 \times 100$) (6)	Illiteracy rate per cent (Col. $5/3 \times 100$) (7)
1951	361	307	56	251	18.3	81.7
1961	439	372	105	267	28.3	71.7
1971	548	458	158	300	34.5	65.5
1981	685	585	256	329	43.7	56.3
1991	846	736	384	352	52.2	47.8

m: million.
Source: *Censuses of India* (various issues).

between Columns 2 and 3 of Table 12.3, the number of such children can be seen to be 54 m in 1951 and 110 m in 1991. Once this young and illiterable population is separated as it should be, and the numbers and percentage of literates and the illiterates among the literables of age five and above are estimated, we get the results as in Columns 4 and 5 in absolute terms and in Columns 6 and 7 in percentage terms. It emerges out that:

(i) Between 1951 and 1991 the number of literates (Column 4) increased from 61 m to 359 m, an addition of 298 m – more than the whole population of Europe.

(ii) The number of illiterates (Column 5) also increased in these years from 246 m to 377 m – i.e. by 131 million.

(iii) The rate of increase of literacy was much higher – 586% in forty years – than the rate of increase of illiteracy – 40% over the same period.

(iv) Literacy percentage rose between 1951 and 1991 from 18% to 52% and illiteracy percentage declined from 82% to 48%.

Even though literacy percentage has been rising and illiteracy percentage declining, the absolute number of illiterates – a staggering 352 m in 1991 compared to 384 m literates – has been seriously dampening the improvement. But it is noteworthy that the scene has changed remarkably in the 1980s and the 1990s (see Figure 12.1).

EDUCATIONAL POVERTY

The phenomenon of poverty also exhibits itself in a lack of education. There may be millions of educated people in India who have never been

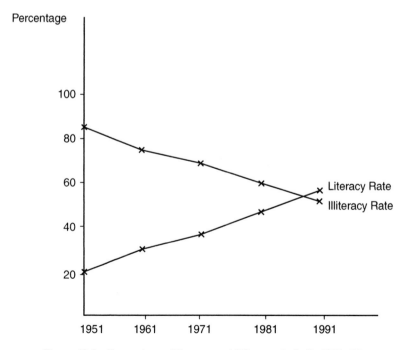

Figure 12.1   Proportions of literates and illiterates in India 1951–91

literate! But in formal terms the completion of high school or higher secondary school education or the obtaining of a university/college degree can be regarded as the hallmark of education. Table 12.4 shows that enrolment at high/higher secondary school stage increased between 1951 and 1993 from 1.48 m to 23.3 m, an increase of 21.82 m or 1474 per cent in 42 years. This enrolment, as a percentage of population in the age group of 14 to 17 years, can be seen to have risen from 4.98 per cent in the earlier year to 27.32 per cent in the later – a fivefold increase – and to 29.52 per cent in 1993 – a sixfold increase. In like manner, as seen in Table 12.5, enrolment in the first degree and higher degree courses increased in these 40 years (1951–91) from 0.17 m to 4.06 m and the percentage of those enrolled in the relevant age group of 18 to 22 years rose from a meagre 0.52 per cent in 1951 to 5.65 per cent in 1991 – a tenfold increase – and to 6.14 per cent in 1993 – a twelvefold increase.

It is true that the enrolled are not exactly the educated of today; but subject to failures and drop-outs they will be the educated of tomorrow – with some questions, of course, about the quality of education. Failures and drop-outs are eliminated if we shift from annual flows of enrolment to the stock of the educated. It is seen in Table 12.6 that the number of matriculates (those who passed out of high schools) increased from 2.8 million in 1951 to 37 million in 1981 (figures for 1991 are not yet available). The matriculates constituted only 0.79 per cent of the total population in the earlier year but came to constitute 5.4 per cent (of a much bigger population) in the later year – approximately a sevenfold increase. The number of graduates is estimated to have increased from 1.18 million in the former year to 15.2 million in the latter. The percentage of graduates to total population was a meagre 0.33 per cent in 1951 but rose to 1.80 per cent in 1991 – a sixfold increase.

What is relevant, however, is not the percentage of the educated to total population but to population in the relevant age groups. As the average age for matriculates is 16–17 and that for obtaining a degree is generally 21–22, the stock percentages should relate to population above these ages. It then turns out from Table 12.6 (Column 2) that between 1951 and 1981 (figures for 1991 are not available) the stock of matriculates increased from 2.8 million to 37.0 million – a thirteenfold increase – and the percentage of that stock to the population above 15 years of age rose from 0.79 to 5.4 per cent. Meanwhile, the number of graduates rose between 1951 to 1991 from 1.18 m to 15.20 m and the percentage of graduates above 22 years increased from 0.84 to 4.20 – nearly a fivefold increase.

Unlike literacy, which may at some time in a nation's history engulf nearly the whole population above a certain age, one does not expect the

Table 12.4
Enrolment in High/Higher Secondary Schools

Year (1)	Population in age group 14–17 years (m) (2)	Enrolment in high/higher secondary schools (m) (3)
1951	29.72	1.48
1961	35.91	3.48
1971	45.51	7.19
1981	59.13	11.28
1991	76.14	20.80
1993	78.93	23.30

Source: Computed on the basis of data contained in *Census Reports* (various issues) and *Annual Reports* of the Ministry of Human Resource Development.

Table 12.5
Enrolment in First Degree and Higher Courses

Year (1)	Population in age group 18–22 years (m) (2)	Enrolment in first degree and higher courses (m) (3)	Enrolment in first degree and higher courses as per cent of population in age 18–22 (Col.3/2 × 100) (Per cent) (4)
1951	33.46	0.17	0.52
1961	39.71	0.56	1.4
1971	49.44	1.95	3.94
1981	66.15	2.75	4.16
1991	71.91	4.06	5.65
1993	74.55	4.58	6.14

Source: Computed on the basis of data contained in *Census Reports* (various issues) and *Annual Reports* of the Ministry of Human Resource Development.

whole population above 17 and 22 years to qualify as matriculates or degree holders, not even in the educationally most advanced societies. Even so, the progress of education in India in accommodating within 30 years a more than 1200 per cent increase in matriculates and within 40 years a 1200 per cent increase in graduates is a real achievement in terms of educational poverty reduction.

Table 12.6
Stock of Educated Persons

Year	Matriculate and above Numbers (m)	Percentage of population above 15 years	Graduates and above Numbers (m)	Percentage of total population	Percentage of population above 22 years
(1)	(2)	(3)	(4)	(5)	(6)
1951	2.80	0.79	1.18	0.33	0.84
1961	8.20	1.90	–	–	–
1971	17.80	3.25	3.31	0.60	1.50
1981	37.00	5.40	7.96	1.16	2.80
1991	NA	NA	15.20	1.80	4.20

Source: Planning Commission, based on *Censuses of Population*.

POVERTY OF HEALTH

Comparable to the nutritional poverty line and the literacy poverty line, what norm can we set up in terms of a health poverty line in order to divide the population between the poor and the non-poor in absolute numbers and as a percentage of the total? It is difficult to classify the population into categories such as healthy and unhealthy. But it is possible to reckon how many people have access to health goods and services which in India – apart from traditional home wisdom – are typically supplied by the state and not obtained through personal expenditures, except in a small measure among the richer categories of population. It is important to construct indicators of access to health measures because after all a decline in death rates in India and a substantial increase in expectations of life at birth has to be explained, not to mention some decline in birth rates. As Table 12.7 indicates, ever since the beginning of the era of planning (1951), while the birth rate has declined from 39.9 per thousand in 1941–51 to 29.5 per thousand in 1981–91, the death rate has come down much more drastically from 27.4 to 9.8 per thousand and the expectation of life at birth for males and females combined has risen from 32.1 to 58.7 years reaching 60.8 years in 1993–4 (see Figure 12.2). As a large and continuous rise in life expectancy must be the result of many factors, these factors have to be identified. In any case, hypotheses and estimations favouring a constant or a rising poverty proportion do not fit the facts of the situation and other measures of access to health have to be evolved. To these we now turn.

One such access to health measure is through the provision of hospital beds. The Seventh Plan Working Group of the Planning Commission

Table 12.7
Birth and Death Rates and Expectation of Life at Birth

Period	Rate per 1000 population		Expectation of life at birth		Combined
	Birth	Death	Males	Females	
(1)	(2)	(3)	(4)	(5)	(6)
1901–11	49.2	42.6	22.6	23.3	22.9
1911–21	48.1	47.2	19.4	20.9	20.1
1921–31	46.4	36.3	26.9	26.6	26.8
1931–41	45.2	31.2	32.1	31.4	31.8
1941–51	39.9	27.4	32.4	31.7	32.1
1951–61	41.7	22.8	41.9	40.6	41.3
1961–71	41.2	19.0	46.4	44.7	45.6
1971–81	37.2	15.0	50.9	50.0	50.5
1981–91	29.5	9.8	58.6	59.0	58.7
1993–94	28.6	9.2	60.4	61.2	60.8

Source: Census of India (various issues) and India's Social Sectors, CMIE, 1996.

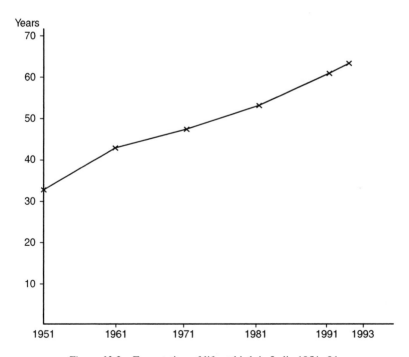

Figure 12.2 Expectation of life at birth in India 1951–91

regarded the level of one bed for thousand population as minimal. This is not a very realistic norm. As morbidity is about 10 per cent of population in any given year, there would be 100 morbid persons per thousand population and these could be served by one bed with an average occupancy of about 3.5 days. However, as only 2 out of 10 patients get actually hospitalized, there are 20 patients out of 100 to be served with one bed. In that case, the average bed occupancy is about 18 days.

Table 12.8 gives the population, the number of beds and the bed-population ratio for the years 1951, 1961, 1971, 1981 and 1991. Applying the normatic bed-population ratio 1 : 100, the absolute number of people covered and not covered by hospital beds is estimated. These numbers are then turned into percentages of total population. The results are also seen in Table 12.8, and in Figure 12.3.

Many more millions of people in urban and rural areas have access to medical facilities of a good, bad or indifferent variety in clinics or as outpatients even if they have no access to hospital beds. Even so, regarding the access to hospital beds as a critical access, it can be seen from

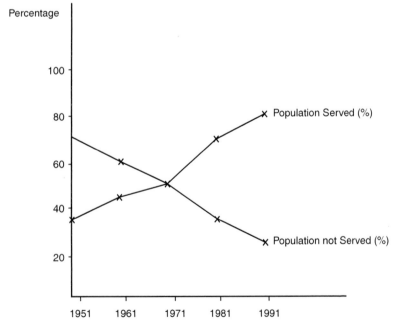

Figure 12.3   Population served by hospital beds in India 1951–91

Table 12.8
Population Served by Hospital Beds

Year	Population	Number of hospital beds (thousand)	Bed population ratio	Population		Percentage of population	
				Served by hospital beds (m)	*Not served by hospital beds (m)*	*Served by hospital beds*	*Not served by hospital beds*
(1)	(m) (2)	(3)	(4)	(5)	(6)	(7)	(8)
1951	361	113	1:3195	113	248	31.3	68.7
1961	439	186	1:2360	186	253	42.4	57.6
1971	548	269	1:2037	269	279	49.1	50.9
1981	685	467	1:1467	467	218	68.2	31.8
1991	846	642	1:1315	642	204	76.0	24.0

Source: Ministry of Health and Family Welfare, *Annual Reports* (various issues).

Table 12.8 that until 1971, those with access were in a minority (49 per cent in 1971), and the absolute number of those having no access was still increasing. But the situation changed drastically during the 1970s and the 1980s. The year 1972 was a year of destiny, as it were, when not only a majority of Indian population began to have access but the absolute number of those without access began to decline. By 1981, 467 m people (68 per cent) were being served and 218 m (32 per cent) were not being served by hospital beds. By 1991, those served by hospital beds had increased to 642 m (76 per cent) and those not served were 204 m (24 per cent). The quality of medical services certainly left a great deal to be desired, though the situation regarding quality was comparable in earlier years as well.

Access to hospital beds is an index favouring urban areas. The major instruments for reducing health poverty in rural areas are the primary health centres (PHC) and the primary health sub-centres (HSC). Run at public expense and involving very little personal expenditure, a PHC is supposed to serve 100 000 people and a HSC 5000 people. But this supposition must be questioned since the quality of Indian health measures is rather poor and access to these measures is much more limited than the health administrators would have us believe. As the norm for the year 2000 is 30 000 persons per PHC, we must reject the figure of 100 000 persons per PHC and allow in our estimation of health access no more than 30 000 persons per PHC. To err on the side of caution, we omit altogether the population served by the HSCs from our estimate of health poverty, even though these HSCs, with a revised yardstick of 4000 persons per sub-centre (not 5000) served about 50 million people in 1961 and no less than 484 million in 1991. The omission of the sub-centres is for the additional reason that many, though not all, of the people who have access to the HSCs also have access to the PHCs. While we do not give credit to the HSCs in our health poverty estimates, we do present in Table 12.10 the data about the number of HSCs and of the people served.

RURAL POPULATION SERVED OR NOT SERVED BY HEALTH CENTRES (HCs)

Table 12.9 shows similar results in terms of access to rural health and medical facilities through primary health centres. By 1981, access to rural health was increasing rapidly, but those without access were also increasing in absolute numbers and were indeed more numerous. Access improved significantly during the 1980s and by 1991 those with access had become 404 million (64 per cent) while those without had declined, even in absolute

Table 12.9
**Rural Population Served/Not Served by
Primary Health Centres (PHCs)**

Year	Rural population	Number of primary health centres	Rural population		Percentage of rural population	
			served by PHCs	not served by PHCs	served by PHCs	not served by PHCs
	(m)		*(m)*	*(m)*		
(1)	(2)	(3)	(4)	(5)	(6)	(7)
1961	360	2565	77	283	21.3	78.7
1971	439	5112	153	286	34.9	65.1
1981	508	7864	236	272	46.5	53.5
1991	623	13464	404	219	64.1	35.1
1995	672	21802	654	18	97.3	2.7

Sources: Computed on the basis of data contained in Census Reports (various issues) and Annual Reports of the Ministry of Health and Family Welfare, Govt. of India (various issues).

Table 12.10
**Rural Population Served/Not Served by
Health Sub-Centres (HSCs)**

Year	Rural population	Number of health sub-centres	Rural population		Percentage of rural population	
			served by HSCs	not served by HSCs	served by HSCs	not served by HSCs
	(m)		*(m)*	*(m)*		
(1)	(2)	(3)	(4)	(5)	(6)	(7)
1961	360	12600	50	310	13.9	86.1
1971	439	28490	114	325	25.9	74.1
1981	526	51191	205	321	39.0	61.0
1991	623	121041	464	139	77.7	22.3
1993	640	131470	526	114	82.2	17.8

Sources: Computed on the basis of data contained in Census Reports (various issues) and Annual Reports of the Ministry of Health and Family Welfare, Govt. of India (various issues).

number, to 219 million (35 per cent). The situation seems to have improved dramatically as, by 1995, the number served by the PHCs had risen to 654 m (97 per cent) and those unserved were only 18 m (2.7 per cent). By all accounts health poverty is sharply on the decline (See Figure 12.4).

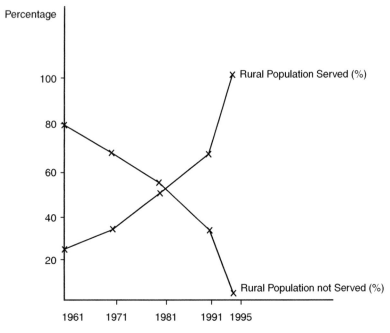

Figure 12.4   Rural population served/not served by Primary Health Centres

A COMPARISON OF DIFFERENT POVERTY LINES IN INDIA

Table 12.11 brings together the estimates of population percentage below various poverty lines in different years from 1951 to 1994. Column 1 gives the percentage of people whose food or calorie consumption is below the accepted norm and is essentially based on the National Sample Survey data. Columns 2 and 5 are our own estimates developed in earlier sections. These show the percentage of illiterates to the total literable population of age five and above, the percentage population in different age groups with no access to education and the percentage of total and rural populations with no access to health and medical facilities.

It is clear that whichever aspect of poverty we examine, the percentage of people below the poverty line is found to have been declining over the years and the percentage of the non-poor has been increasing. Even the absolute numbers of the poor have begun to decline as far as the poverty of illiteracy and the poverty of health is concerned. It is also clear that the decline of poverty proportions is a phenomenon that is common to consumption of goods and services through personal expenditures and through access to public goods and services, but the role of the latter turns out to be quite conspicuous.

As is well known, a wide range of goods and services such as food, education and health care, are targeted for the benefit of the poor and are provided by the government for the benefit of the poor at highly subsidized prices. When such subsidized goods and services are also taken into account (as these are not reflected in personal income and consumption based poverty estimation), the incidence of different forms of poverty would be even smaller than that indicated above. The trend in the allocation of resources for major social services such as education and health care shows a rising trend. For instance, educational allocation has increased from 2.17 per cent to 3 per cent of GDP during 1974–5 to 1994–5. The corresponding allocations for health services were 0.85 per cent and 1.17 per cent (Table 12.11, page 132).

Likewise, Table 12.12 (page 133) shows that the per capita expenditure on various social services has increased from Rs 44 in 1974–5 to Rs 557 in 1995–6 (i.e. thirteen times in the last two decades). The total expenditure on social services as a share of GDP has increased from 3.9 to 6.2 per cent during the above period. Clearly, even after accounting for inflation, the benefits derived by the people out of individual income and consumption as well as the subsidized goods and services offered by the government have considerably improved – which indicates a diminution in all forms of poverty.

THE TRICKLE-DOWN EFFECT

Probing into the immediate future, as stated earlier, an important development can be discerned. In the first 25 years of planned development a 3.5 per cent per annum increase of the national product was eaten up to the tune of about 2.3 per cent by population growth. The net improvement in per capita income of a little more than 1 per cent was too small to involve the poor in the growth process and pull them up above the poverty line. In other words, economic growth was not trickling down – unlike countries such as South Korea, Thailand, Malaysia and Indonesia where, owing to at least 6 per cent growth in the national product and a 3 per cent population growth, there was at least a 3 per cent rise in per capita income, and hence the trickle-down process was much more effective. That is why India was running a host of anti-poverty programmes in the hope that if economic growth was not uplifting the poor, the programmes would. However, it is now clear that in the foreseeable future, as in the last twenty years,

Table 12.11
Proportion of Population Below Different Poverty Lines

Year	Nutritional poverty No. of the poor (mn.)	Expenditure based poverty Percentage of population	NNP per capita at 1980–81 prices (Rs.)	Index (1951=100)	Illiteracy rate	Educational poverty Enrolment ratios by levels Primary 6–11 yrs.	Middle 11–14 yrs.	Secondary 11–17 yrs.	Health poverty Population not covered by health facilities General	Rural	Life expectancy
(1)	(2)	(3)	(4)	(5)	(6)	(7)	(8)	(9)	(10)	(11)	(12)
1951	186.0	51.5	1127	100.0	81.7	56.9	87.9	94.7	68.7	–	32.1
1961	240.1	54.7	1350	119.8	71.7	37.6	77.6	–	57.6	78.7	41.3
1971	274.1	45.1	1520	134.9	65.5	23.6	65.8	79.2	50.9	55.1	45.6
1981	271.0	37.4*	1630	144.6	56.3	19.5	58.1	71.4	31.8	45.1	50.4
1991	159.3	18.5	2222	197.2	47.8	–1.1	39.9	53.9	24.0	35.2	58.7
1994	177.2***	18.9**	2292	203.4	–	–3.0	34.5	–	NA	2.7@@	61.0@

Source: Compiled from various tables presented in this report.
* Pertains to 1983.
** Pertains to 1993–94.
*** Pertains to 1992.
@ for 1992.
@ @ Pertains to 1995.

Table 12.12
**Expenditure on Social Services* by the
Centre and State Governments**

Year	Per capita expenditure (Rs)	Social service expenditure as % of govt.'s budget	Social service expenditure as % of GDP
(1)	(2)	(3)	(4)
1974–5	44.4	16.7	3.9
1980–1	93.2	17.3	5.2
1990–1	364.5	17.5	5.6
1995–6**	556.8	16.2	6.2

* Includes education, public health, water supply and sanitation, family welfare, housing and urban development, relief for natural calamities, social security and welfare.
** Budget estimates.
Source: Computed on the basis of data contained in *Public Finance: India's Centre and State Governments*, CMIE, June, 1996.

a 5 per cent growth of India's national product (7 per cent in 1995 and 1996), together with a mere 2 per cent increase in the population, would bring about a net per capita growth of 3 per cent per year and this ought to raise standards of living for the poor much more than in the past.

On top of all this, if India's massive anti-poverty programmes – such as the Integrated Rural Development Programme (IRDP), the National Rural Employment Programme (NREP), Nehru Rozgar Yojana and the like – become more effective that would provide another reason why the poverty proportion should decline even faster than in the recent past. The upshot clearly is that the old notion of a chronic persistence of poverty both in absolute and percentage terms has to be given up and alternative method-ologies of poverty estimation, such as the Human Development Index, focusing on the total quality of life rather than calorie or food consump-tion, and including the consumption of public goods rather than personal expenditures alone, have to be evolved.

Part III
Some Solutions for Poverty Removal

13 How Recession in the Asian Economies Negatively Impacts the Poverty Situation

While the progress of the East Asian and South-East Asian economies was more or less undisturbed during the 1980s and the 1990s and tended almost linearly to reduce poverty levels, a sudden cataclysm gripped these economies and, in particular, the East Asian Economies of the ASEAN countries, Korea and Japan, and sent these economies spiralling downwards into a deep recession. Many macro and micro variables showed a sudden decline and the fundamentals of these economies suffered quite seriously from their negative impact. Even China could not be excluded from a decline in some of the fundamentals though many other variables remained steady in their magnitude. The Far Eastern shock had unfavourable consequences on the economies of South Asia though the damage was somewhat limited, as in the case of India. But the negative impact of the crisis spread far beyond South Asia and reached even the United States, Western Europe and Australia. There was a slow-down in the exports of these countries to the South-East Asian markets owing to a decline in the purchasing power of the latter. The export capabilities of South-East Asian countries were also reduced considerably owing to a decline in their production and a disorientation of their banking mechanism, and this caused a serious fall in the two-way trade between the East and the West. Though a full evaluation of the impact of declining fundamentals in the Far East has not yet been calculated, it is obvious that the continuing and deepening recession there has worsened the poverty situation and transferred millions of people from the zone of affluence to the zone of poverty. Such crucial variables as income generation, industrial production, banking services, educational levels and health levels have all been affected negatively.

ROBUST TRENDS BEFORE 1997

For some years before 1997, the growth rates of the Far Eastern economies had been hovering at a trend rate between 6 and 10 per cent per annum.

Earlier, Japan had demonstrated a growth rate between 10 and 12 per cent in its GNP for more than a dozen years continuously. China also has had a growth rate well above 10 per cent and even India, a relatively sluggish performer in GDP growth of about 5 per cent per annum, had gone up to a 7 per cent growth in two successive years 1995 and 1996. The export growth of the South-East Asian as well as the South Asian economies had also been robust in the pre-1997 period and even India had left its sluggish export growth behind and reached a figure of 20 per cent annual growth in its exports. Imports of these economies were also rising *pari passu* and capital goods imports too were flourishing.

With the growth of GNP/GDP and the growth of exports and imports proceeding at a robust rate, employment in these countries was rising and there was no gainsaying a rise in prosperity and a decline in poverty. Japan had become a strong export competitor of the United States and Europe and all those economies importing automobiles, electronic goods and technological items were concerned about the flood of Japanese exports and the strengthening of the Japanese *yen*. Industrial production had been on the increase in the South-East Asian and South Asian countries. While India, to take one instance, had been registering a GDP growth of 7 per cent and an 8 to 10 per cent industrial growth per annum, Chinese output and exports were rising along with Japan, the ASEAN economies and Korea.

POST-1997 COLLAPSE

Then, in 1997, suddenly, came the collapse and the major economic variables in Eastern economies went into a tailspin. The domestic currencies plummeted in relation to the dollar and West European currencies and in the circumstances were either devalued or depreciated through market forces. The GDP and industrial production growth slowed down, leading to a sharp fall in exports. The banking system faced a serious situation, and export financing became difficult. These economies were truly in an unexpected recession. The shock was too sudden and those in charge of the management of these economies were unable to cope.

The decline in the foreign exchange values of the domestic currencies of South-East Asia and South Asia was unbelievable. The countries designated as 'Asian Tigers' were now looking for cover, first, to steady themselves and, subsequently, to prevent further decline in the economic variables. Between June 1997 and June 1998, the currencies of Japan, Indonesia, Malaysia, Thailand, Philippines and Korea all fell by large percentages, and even China experienced a decline in its external currency value.

Compared to the GDP growth in 1996, the 1998 growth had either slowed or became negative in all these economies.

Compared to the Far Eastern currencies, between mid-1996 and mid-1998 the Indian rupee probably experienced a comparatively small decline, nevertheless, a disturbing one, from Rs 39 per dollar to Rs 42.50 per dollar, and India's growth rate of GDP too showed a relatively small reduction from 7 per cent to 5 per cent growth. India's industrial production in the same period slowed down from 8 per cent growth to 4.2 per cent growth and Indian exports fell from an approximately 20 per cent rise per annum to a little more than 3 per cent increase.

The depressing scenario which has been developing in 1997 and 1998 in the economies of the Far East is being reported almost daily in the major newspapers and other media. The general tendency between mid-1997 and mid-1998 has been for the recession to deepen and the fundamentals of nearly all the Far Eastern economies, including China and Japan, to weaken perceptibly. The United States, the most robust of the Western economies, has left the recession behind and has been growing in each quarter during this period at an annual rate of between 3 and 4 per cent. The European economies, in general, remained in recessionery circumstances at least a year longer than the United States, but seemed to be going into a recovery during 1998. This recovery applies to several basic variables, but not employment. The prolonged recession in the West, by reducing or slowing the purchasing power of the West (and Japan) has reduced the imports of products from the Far East and South Asia. This in fact, has been one of the complex causal factors in the East Asian and South Asian recession, though the causality goes beyond the mere impact of recession in the West.

Even as the fundamentals are weakening in the Far East, the main villain of the piece is the growing unemployment, and it is this variable that negatively impacts poverty more than anything else and transfers a growing slice of the population from prosperity to poverty. As the phenomenon is too recent to have been researched upon and analysed fully in professional literature, the following reports in the *International Herald Tribune*, from mid-1997 to mid-1998, about different countries, underline the grim happenings during the march of the recession within this period – which finally converge in unemployment and the emergence of poverty.

THE SOUTH-EAST ASIAN RECESSION

An IMF report forecast that the three economies most affected by the Asian crisis would diminish this year (1998): Indonesia would contract by 0.5 per cent, Thailand by 3.1 per cent and South Korea by 0.8 per cent. For Japan, the IMF is forecasting zero growth this year, a sharp revision of its projection four months ago of 4.1 per cent growth. Mr. Moossa (of the IMF) warned that even zero growth 'may not materialize' this year.

(*International Herald Tribune*, 14 April 1998)

Japan

'Japan is probably already in a recession and its economy is unlikely to show signs of economic growth until the second half of this year', the International Monetary Fund said.

' The Japanese economy probably contracted in the first quarter of this year (1998) and will, probably, contract again the second quarter' said Mr. Michael Moossa, the Fund's Chief Economist.

' To sustain growth', he said, 'Tokyo, probably, must plan on fiscal stimulus measures in 1999 that go beyond the Dollar 75 billion package of public spending and tax cuts introduced last week'.

The Fund said the global effects of the crisis would very likely be 'more severe' than initially forecast. It revised its world economic growth forecast for 1998 to 3.1 per cent, down from its forecast of 4.3 per cent six months ago'.

Although the IMF said the turmoil that erupted last year in Asia had abated since January (1998), it warned in its twice-annual world economic outlook that 'considerable uncertainty remains about the resolution of the crisis and its global repercussions'.

(*International Herald Tribune*, 14 April 1998)

As the Japanese economy is moving deep into recession it was announced by a Minister of Government that even a 4 trillion yen cut from Japanese income-tax in a plan to pump 10 trillion yen into the economy failed to bolster the yen.

Japan's unemployment rate rose to a record 3.6 per cent in February (1998). The number of unemployed reached 2.46 million, up 16,000 from a year earlier. It is the highest unemployment rate since Tokyo started compiling data in 1953. A large fall-off in public works projects and depressed consumer spending pushed up the number of workers who lost their jobs, an official said.

The job-to-applicants-ratio seen by many economists as a better indication of future employment conditions, fell to 0.61 in February from 0.64 in January (1998), meaning there were 61 job openings for over 100 job seekers. It was the lowest level since January 1987.

The Standard & Poors Corp. cut the credit ratings of the Bank of Tokyo Mitsubishi Limited, the worlds biggest bank, as well as the rating of three other Japanese banks. Standard & Poors said profits were getting squeezed by a sluggish economy and billions of dollars in bad loans.

(*International Herald Tribune*, 14 April 1998)

Sandra Sugawara stated in the *International Herald Tribune* (14 April 1998):

Any hope that Japan could be the engine of growth to revive other struggling Asian economies has largely been abandoned giving way to the notion that Japan's economy could spiral downwards so quick that it could plunge Asia into another economic tailspin, according to many economists .... The economy will very likely turn in its worst performance in almost a quarter century in the year ending 31st March, many economists said. The figures led even Tokyo to admit that its minimal growth target of 0.1 per cent for the year might be too optimistic. The economy was brought down by a series of tax increases and bankruptcies that prompted consumers to save more and spend less and with exports to Asia slumping, companies are cutting capital spending, leading to declines in output, jobs and wages. Few companies anticipate a rapid turn around ....

Economists worry that Japan is about to get caught up in a vicious cycle where lower demand for products causes prices to fall, which, in turn, causes even lower demand. They warn that Japan, the world's second largest economy, is about to enter the worst deflationary period in decades.

China

China, which has been relatively immune to contagion from the crisis, is, nonetheless, forecast to see its growth slowed down to about 7 per cent this year, compared with 8.8 per cent in 1997. Edward Steinfeld, Professor at

Massachusetts Institute of Technology, wrote in *International Herald Tribute* of 28–29 March 1998:

> The irony of the Asian financial crisis is that China, seemingly least involved, is about to suffer the most monumental consequences. Events in East Asia have constantly driven home to Beijing the costs of inappropriate bank loaning and capital mis-location – Reforms put off for years, even decades, are now being carried out in rapid-fire succession. China's currency is not convertible on world markets and domestic firms carry very little foreign denominated data. But deeper lessons regarding the hazards of accumulated bad loans and the potential for financial collapse have begun to register in Beijing.
>
> The Central Government ordered individual banks to extend 'policy loans' – non-commercial giveaways – to specific state enterprises. Local governments pressured state banks to infuse favored firms with 'soft' loans. The upshot overtime has been a thorough undermining of the nation's banking system. In essence, national investment resources – household savings, have been systematically directed to non-viable firms. ... Levels of non-performing debt in the system estimated conservatively at 5% of the GDP are even higher than those of China's troubled East Asian neighbors. To put it simply, the Chinese banking system is currently insolvent. The country's fiscal resources are insufficient for setting up any sort of comprehensive social safety net. Workers are being cut lose and precious little is in place, institutionally, to catch them when they fall.

Hong Kong

Philip Segal wrote in the *International Herald Tribune* of 21 July 1998:

> Unemployment [in Hong Kong] rose to a 15 year high at 4.5% here in April through June (1998) .... 'The impact of the Asian financial crisis is much more widespread and protracted for the whole region than any one could have expected', said Donald Tsand, the Hong Kong Financial Secretary .... The employment statistics, showing the 5th monthly increase in a row from 4.1% in the March–May (1998) period, add to a depressing array of economic numbers reported in recent months. The economy is shrinking, down by about 2% in the first quarter of the year, compared with a year earlier according to government estimates. Retail sales have fallen off a cliff dropping 14.7% in April (1998) compared with April 1997. As the economy slows, companies continue to lay off

workers. The number of unemployed has doubled since early last autumn to 144,000 in a population of six million ... 'There isn't any light at the end of the tunnel on unemployment', said the chief economist at Clarion Security Asia Limited.

Indonesia

Michael Richardson writing in the *International Herald Tribune* of 21 July 1998, highlights the impact of the recession on poverty:

Indonesia is the fourth most populous country in the world. It has a work force of about 90 million people. At least 20 million of them are expected to lose their jobs in the next 12 months. In the same 12 months, the government expects the number of people living below the official poverty line to increase to nearly 96 million – almost half of the population. Many parents have already been forced to take their children out of school. Among numerous people in the predicament, the author cites as an example the case of Mohammad Illyas and wife, Noni, who have to decide whether to keep two of their sons and their daughter in school or take them out ... After Indonesia's currency, the rupiah, collapsed, millions of Indonesians lost their jobs. Illyas too was dismissed after eight years as a casual laborer in the port of Jakarta. When that job went, a monthly income that averaged 300,000 rupiah (now about Dollars 23) which was just enough to house, food, cloth and educate his six children was lost. To keep his children in the government school this year, Illyas will need an equivalent of at least two month's income at his former pay level.

SOME EXTERNAL EFFECTS OF THE SOUTH-EAST ASIAN CRISIS

The impact of the June (1998) crisis on North America and Western Europe will be mild, (an IMF report said), with an improved anti-inflation effect that could even help to reduce the risk of over-heating in the US economy.

The Fund upgraded its forecast slightly for the US predicting 2.9% growth in 1998 and 2.2% next year. The European Union, now enjoying a spreading recovery, was forecast to grow by 2.8% both this year (1998) and next. Among the big continental economies, France will lead the pack in 1998 with 2.9% growth, the Fund said, while Germany will

expand 2.5% and Italy 2.3%. Economic growth in Britain will slow to
2.3% from 3.3% in 1997, it said.

The IMF said that spillovers from the Asian crisis had been most
apparent in Russia, Ukraine and Estonia. Russia's economy will grow
just 1% in 1998, the IMF said ... countries in transition from Communism
will grow by an average 2.9% this year ... down from its forecast six
months ago of 4.2%. The Fund's prediction for African growth was lowered to 4.6% from 5% and that for the Middle East to 3% from 4.2%.

(*International Herald Tribune*, 14 April 1998)

France

The number of job seekers fell in February (1998) by 7300 to
30,26,400. But France's unemployment rate was unchanged at 12.1%,
the Labor Ministry said. A gradual improvement has slowly reduced the
number of people unemployed and looking for work in France for the
past year and trimmed the jobless rate by 4/10ths of a percentage point.
'We have an economic recovery in France that allows some job creation, but it is not strong enough to lead to a marked reduction in unemployment. I do not think we will go below 12% unemployment scene',
said an Economist at Credit Lyonnais. Parliament passed a Bill that
would cut a legal work week to 35 hours without a pay cut, by 2000.
Business leaders opposed the Bill saying that it will lead to higher costs
and job losses.

(Reuters AP cited by *International Herald Tribune*, March 1998)

Germany

The German construction industry plans to cut 70,000 jobs this year
[1998] because of the sector's poor prospects, the ZDB building industry association said, according to a Reuters report from Bonn. It said
40,000 of the jobs were expected to be lost in Western Germany.

(*International Herald Tribune*, March 1998)

14 What Obstructs and What Facilitates Poverty Removal

POVERTY INCREASES DURING THE INITIAL PHASES OF GROWTH

It has been noted in many economic and statistical analyses that when stagnant economies are subjected to the process of economic growth and begin to leave their stagnation behind, overall growth is often accompanied by a maldistribution of income and, consequently, by a maldistribution of wealth. This is often the case because the beneficiaries of the growth process are almost invariably the active agents in the process – the entrepreneurs, the manufacturers, the farmers who have surpluses to sell, the traders, the exporters and the importers. That is to say, the economically resilient members of the society who come to participate actively in the growth process, also come to receive the benefits. The other less resilient and non-participating members who often constitute the large bulk of the society get left behind. There are generally very large numbers of them and they constitute by far the larger proportion of the population. There are perhaps very few societies in the world – perhaps none – in earlier as well as in more recent centuries which have passed through the process of the economic growth without a maldistribution of income and wealth, at any rate in the initial decades of the process.

It is also true that the process of economic growth, again almost invariably, is accompanied by inflation and there seem to be very few societies which have moved from stagnation to economic growth without inflation. This is because the process of economic growth is almost always accompanied by a shift of resources in favour of investment – that is to say, a shift in favour of saving and capital formation rather than consumption. This preference for investment can be caused by any of the numerous factors that ignite the process of economic growth – the discovery of new mineral or other resources, some major inventions or innovations, such as the steam engine or electricity, some returns from colonial domination invested back home, the emergence of new leadership encouraging savings, investment and growth such as Calvin's, Martin Luther's or Mahatma Gandhi's, some structural change in the methods and practices of society such as the emergence of Protestant ethics, or some mass migration of resilient groups in the population. Whatever be the cause or causes, the end result is often a shift of resources in favour of investment.

As investment begins, the recipients of the investment flow save their share out of their earnings and spend a proportion according to their propensity to spend; and those who receive in the second round save their part and spend the balance ... and so on. This, as is well-known, leads to the multiplier process which ends up in an increase in national income as a multiple of the original investment and depends on the value of the multiplier – which is the reciprocal of the marginal propensity to save of the society in question. This process enhances effective demand and has an inflationary potential. While the process of income generation and hence demand generation begins almost simultaneously with investment and reaches its full effect within a short span of time, the same investment tends to generate supply by delayed action, so to speak, as the gestation period between additional investment and additional supplies emerging out of it are very long. Thus it happens that the demand-generating effect of investment normally runs ahead of the supply-generating effect of the same investment and this lag in supplies results in price increases, almost invariably. It therefore comes about that inflation becomes an integral part of the economic growth process, at any rate in the earlier stages until the supply mechanism catches on vigorously. This is the reason why there are almost no examples of sustained economic growth in developing countries without inflation.

It is thus clear that even as economic growth rarely occurs without an initial maldistribution of income, so there are also hardly any examples of economic growth occurring without inflation. Now, as the process of inflation itself is maldistributive in nature – maldistributive of income and wealth in favour of manufacturers, surplus farmers, traders and debtors and against workers, consumers and creditors – the maldistribution of income and wealth is sharpened through inflation itself. Poverty enhancement is thus an obvious initial outcome. In other words, one can sum up this complex phenomenon by stating that periods of economic growth are periods of maldistribution; periods of economic growth are also periods of inflation; and periods of inflation are almost invariably periods of maldistribution of income and wealth – and hence of poverty increase.

It follows that during periods of economic growth, especially in the earlier phases, poverty tends to increase until, much later, the benefits of the growth process in terms of enhanced real wages and real incomes begin to reach the bulk of the people – and this can happen only when the benefits of mass-produced consumption goods become accessible to the masses of the population.

SLOW GROWTH DOES NOT TRICKLE DOWN INTO THE POVERTY ZONE

A variant of the aforementioned process is that economic growth in the early stages and at slow rates does not trickle down easily to the masses of the population and tends to remain confined to the elite society of producers, traders and active agents in the market place. This, however, is not an absolute statement and examples exist where the trickle-down of economic growth does take place as well as where it does not. For instance, in Korea, Taiwan and the ASEAN countries economic growth rates have hovered in the region of 6–10 per cent or even higher per annum over extended periods. Population growth rates have been around 3 per cent per annum and, in consequence, the per capita growth rates have been as high as 3–6 per cent or more. That kind of a rather high per capita growth seems to percolate down to the masses and involve them in economic activity. The phenomenon of maldistribution of income and wealth does not seem to be so glaring under these circumstances since the poorer segments of the population are not left out or left behind in the growth process. This is the reason why these countries preferred to press on with the growth process itself, sometimes through the State mechanism but often through the market forces, and did not have to operate major 'programmes' of economic uplift as some other countries with weaker growth did.

On the other hand, there are countries like India where the growth rate of output was around 3.5 per cent per annum on an average, between 1950 and 1975, while the population growth was between 2.4 and 2.2 per cent. Thus, the net per capita growth remained between 1.1 and 1.3 per cent per annum. Such a meagre and sluggish per capita growth does not seem to trickle down and huge masses of the population do not get involved in new (or old) economic activities. Owing to this non-involvement of a great mass of rural and urban people in gainful work – while the top layers of the society are doing rather well for themselves – maldistribution of income becomes the order of the day and poverty fails to be controlled and reduced. Such a lack of trickle-down of economic growth in sluggishly growing economies is the main reason why the managers and decision makers in these economies decide to organize 'programmes' of economic development and poverty reduction. They hope that if growth does not percolate and reduce poverty, the programmes will. Hence, in those countries we get a surfeit of anti-poverty programmes as well as developmental programmes. In the case of India, there has been the Community Development Programme (CDP), the Intensive Agricultural District Programme (IADP), the Integrated Rural Development Programme (IRDP), the National Rural Employment Programme (NREP), the Nehru Rozgar Yojana (NRY) and several others, all as a substitute for the non-trickle-down effect of economic growth.

However, around 1975 or so, the economic growth rate of India caught up with other Asian economies and moved into higher figures. During the 5th, 6th and 7th Plans (1975–80, 1980–5 and 1985–90 respectively) the growth rate was measured at about 5 per cent per year. Meanwhile, population growth slowed down owing to various factors ranging from general literacy (particularly female), improved education and health services and the use of contraceptives, vasectomy, tubectomy, leprascopy and several other methods of family planning, and settled in the region of 2 per cent per annum. The net per capita growth in India then rose, for the first time, to about 3 per cent per year. At that figure, per capita growth does seem to trickle down to the masses and involves them much more in economic activity, as happened in South Korea, Taiwan and the ASEAN countries. That seems to be one of the major reasons why, after hovering around a static situation of about 48 per cent of the population, the numbers below poverty line in India have been declining and are estimated to be around 18.9 per cent of the population, according to one estimation, and 39 per cent, according to another. In any case, as recent data reveal, the average life span (or life expectation at birth) is now turning out to be as high as 61 years compared to 50 in 1981. This situation augurs well for poverty reduction in India in the coming years as poverty-stricken people are getting more involved in the growth process and the indicators of progress are also revealing the same tendency.

THE TRICKLE-DOWN PROCESS

It appears from the economic history of developing economies in the past half-century that economic growth cannot, and does not, trickle down into the poverty zones of a country so long as economic controls, regulations, rationing systems, quotas, import controls, export controls, capital issues controls, foreign exchange controls and a host of other controls continue to be the order of the day. To be fair, however, a controlled economy, a command economy or a semi-command economy, may be different in that it starts with the best of intentions to reach the poor and endeavours to provide them with employment, income, health facilities, housing, literacy, education and other amenities such as food distribution systems. These programmes do bring about a change in the direction of poverty reduction to some extent. But at the end of the day, it appears that policy intentions are fulfilled to only a limited extent. As the negative aspects of over-regulation and over-control take over from the positive effects, the disabilities of the control systems for ordinary citizens begin to more than outweigh the benefits and achievements, and the positive intentions of planning and public policy are virtually washed away.

The difficulty with controlled and semi-controlled economies is that these focus basically on demand management and not so much on supply augmentation. As supplies of food and essential goods and services are generally short to begin with, the controlled regimes become preoccupied with distributing the limited supplies better. This leads to price controls, rationing systems, quotas and other restrictions. It is a well-known characteristic of a price-controlled economy with physical controls that the urge to supply more does not exist. Price controls in particular reduce the incentive on the part of the producers to produce more, as these controls violate one of the basic laws of economics – that at a price lower than the market price (which is what a controlled price is) suppliers will supply less. As price controls cause a dwindling of supplies – even if they distribute the existing supplies better – the economy does not go into the zone of greater availability of goods and lower prices. It tends to get stuck with shortages and high prices. A controlled economy, in other words, turns out to be a shortage economy. It does not pay enough attention to supply augmentation and concentrates basically on a better distribution of poverty! Controls, therefore, have a habit of perpetuating the shortages. Under a controlled regime, as the suppliers do not have the incentive to supply more, the day never comes when supplies are augmented and price controls and rationing become unnecessary and could be abolished.

Price controls and physical controls have also a characteristic of spreading from commodity to commodity and, in due course, bring into the network of controls numerous items which it was never the intention of the political regime to invoke. A shortage economy may impose price and quality controls and decide to do so only on a few essential commodities such as food grains, kerosene oil, mill cloth and essential medicines, and might even plan to remove the controls as supplies increase. But this actually never happens and various controls not only create more shortages and perpetuate themselves but also spread to numerous other commodities – so much so that, say, ten years later when an analyst looks at the controlled system, it turns out that the controls have proliferated extensively and that instead of the 20 original controls, there may actually be 250 other items in the network of control.

Such a network of controls has a dynamic of its own. As controls create and multiply the shortages, there is a strong tendency on the part of the population, especially of the high-income variety, to offer a price higher than the controlled price prevailing in the rationing system. With price offers outside the controlled markets, higher than the controlled price, the suppliers and the sellers move away from supplying to the rationing system and strike deals with those who offer free-market prices – which are now declared illegal or 'black market' prices. When the numerous micro-dealings in various commodities and services at black market prices are summed up together, there emerges a huge volume of black earnings obtained from illegal sales at illegal prices.

Now, an important characteristic of such black earnings is that they cannot be declared to the administrative and fiscal authorities for fear of penal action; nor can they be invested in transparent institutional arrangements such as the purchase of bonds, debentures or equity shares in the stock markets. The result is that neither does the government of the day get any taxes from the undeclared, illegal receipts, nor does capital formation occur through contributions to stocks and shares. These black earnings then are an enemy of income redistribution even as they are enemies of economic growth. In this maldistributed set-up, anti-poverty mechanisms become the major casualty and prosperity is confined to the elite society consisting of producers, traders, black marketers, exporters, importers and the richer consumers.

The dynamics of over-control and over-regulation not only deal a body-blow to anti-poverty programmes but they eventually involve the controlled economies in various crises such as those of foreign exchange, budgetary shortfalls, infrastructural shortages and, in general, a crisis of supplies. In a demand-managed economy replete with quantitative controls and price and wage controls, the producers hardly have any incentives and freedoms. What to produce, how much to produce, when to produce, where to produce, with what techniques to produce and how much capacity to build – all these matters come to be determined by bureaucrats and politicians who are probably not qualified to take these decisions. The result is an inadequacy of supplies and a regime of shortages and black markets. The basic point emerges that in such regimes the population living in the poverty zone neither receives the benefits of abundantly supplied and mass-produced goods and services at affordable prices, nor do they benefit from scale economies and low-cost goods and services which are continually enlarging in volumes and continually improving in their technical efficiency.

The crises mentioned here, which finally emerge in a command or a semi-command economy, have often led to a hue and cry and ultimately to a desire on the part of consumers, producers, exporters, importers and other productive agents for an alternative system of liberalization, decontrol, delicensing and deregulation which would strengthen the market forces, enlarge the areas of free market operations and contract the size of the controlled economy. In fact, in the last few years, there has been a wave in most developed countries towards liberalizing and globalizing programmes of economic development. Partly prodded by international institutions like the World Bank and the IMF, and partly analysing their own economic misfortunes and the failures of economic policies, many regimes in the world have opted for cuts in government expenditures, a reduction in tax rates, both direct and indirect, a cut in fiscal deficits, a reduction of controls, delicensing of industry, a free-market determination of the rate of exchange of the domestic currency (instead of letting these rates be determined by bureaucrats), a switch from import-substitution strategies to export-generating arrangements and freer flow of foreign investment with a view to importation of technologies from the owners of these technologies abroad. This set of measures, almost the opposite of the hitherto prevailing set-up, goes under the name of structural adjustment programme and has been in vogue intensively since the end of the decade of 1980s.

STRUCTURAL ADJUSTMENT PROGRAMMES AS A METHOD FOR THE ELIMINATION OF POVERTY

Governments of many developing countries have adopted these structural adjustment programmes in different degrees. Countries like India have altered their budgetary and fiscal policies in favour of a consistent and continuous tax rate reduction in income-tax, corporate tax, excise duties and customs duties and have combined this fiscal change with an attempt to reduce the monetary deficits and fiscal deficits as a proportion of the GDP. They have also allowed the rate of the local currency in relation to other hard currencies to be determined in the market place through the forces of supply and demand rather than let the rates be decided by bureaucrats in the Ministries of Finance and the Central Banks. Together with this change, these regimes have liberalized their policies towards the import of goods and services and have become supporters of the importation of technology from abroad. While planning to handle their balances of payment better, these countries have liberalized the flow of foreign capital – both direct foreign capital and capital flows from foreign financial institutions into domestic industries through the stock markets. Moreover, some of these countries have virtually removed the licensing systems which earlier forced domestic corporate enterprises to queue for licences to expand capacity or to start a new line of enterprise. This liberalization and freedom to expand, contract, open new lines or close old lines of business, has been lauded substantially by the domestic industrialists and businessmen and has been seen as a major reform.

While the benefits of these reforms, together with some shortcomings, are now coming to light gradually, it has been debated hotly whether these reforms, which amount to substituting a market economy in place of a controlled economy, have anything to do with poverty reduction and employment generation for the masses of the people. The key questions to be faced by the protagonists of market-oriented policies are whether the market economy has a large redistributive potential in favour of the poor; whether its focus on high-powered technology and imports of capital-intensive items will not compromise the employment of manpower and whether large – and poorer – segments of the societies will not be left high and dry as the benefits of the new reform are confined to the manufacturers, traders, exporters, importers and the richer consumers? In other words, the basic issue is whether the new economic growth generated through structural adjustment programmes and market orientation will trickle down to the masses and initially reduce and finally eliminate poverty?

It would seem from economic logic as well as from some early effects of structural adjustment policies that, with some modifications, these policies have a great deal of potential for poverty reduction and elimination. Though the mechanism and the path through which a market economy abolishes poverty has never been spelt out in policy making circles, it is worth while reflecting upon this possibility, both in economic logic and in the recent effects of structural reform in some countries. There is at least one possible route through which a market-oriented strategy can eventually eliminate poverty. The first step is to remove oligopolies – a few large market-dominating and non-competing producers – and allow a larger number of entries of producers in each commodity, at any rate in the major commodities. The existing situation has been oligopolistic as licences are given only to very few producers in each product. It might well be that while there are 20 producers in the market for a given commodity, 17 of them account for only 10 per cent of the product, the remaining three having a share of 20 per cent, 30 per cent and 40 per cent in the market for that particular product. As oligopolies are seldom interested in the expansion of volumes but aim at a higher price, the product does not expand much in an oligopolistic set-up. An oligopoly believes that as it is itself a very large operator with, say, a 30 per cent share in the market, the expansion of its product by, say, 20 per cent, will shake up the market and will reduce the price of the product against it. In that case, it believes that while it will gain additional revenue from additional production, it will lose more than that owing to the lowering of price – which will have been caused by its own action to increase production. Thus, as years go by and oligopolies perpetuate themselves, output seldom increases by any impressive amount and prices seldom decline.

Hence, an imperative step in the new policies is to remove the licensing system and bring in as many producers as would like to join in a given line of industry. It may well be that within five years, there may be 20 competitive producers instead of three oligopolists. Once entry brings in a larger number of producers, the next development would be an increase in the degree of competition amongst them. This competition would ensure greater efficiency among the competitors and would lead them to improve existing technologies, import new technologies, train their human material better, provide a far better management and attempt generally to enlarge the size of the operations, obtain scale economies and cut costs. In this competitive situation, those who can adjust themselves well would survive and the rest would have a tendency to collapse and go out of business – perhaps switching over to other lines of business from the present one.

However, before the firms which are unable to compete effectively collapse and get out of the particular line of industry, there will certainly emerge a tendency for such firms to want to merge or amalgamate with the more successful ones, even as there will arise an urge among the successful firms to take over the weaker firms. In the current set-up, in many developing countries, one can observe the process of mergers, amalgamation and takeovers in progress. One of the outcomes of this process is that as 20 firms merge into, say, 12, the scale of operations of the resultant firms gets enlarged and the enlarged scale goes on to reduce the cost of production per unit along a declining average cost curve.

When the efficient and cost-effective arrangements, which competition enforces, are combined with the economies of scale which amalgamation and larger-sized operations bring, the stage is set for a considerable cut in the cost of production. The impact of the incoming new technologies is also in the direction of cost cutting. All new technologies involve higher costs *in absolute terms* but if combined with efficient managements nearly all of them lead to lower costs *per unit of output*. This powerful combination of various cost reductions obviously generates larger demand by far, and larger demand leads to larger production and still lower costs along the declining cost curve.

Meanwhile, as the low-cost firms which emerge as successful in the competitive regime begin to produce at a large scale with effective scale economies, improved technologies and professional management, their profitability increases. Widespread profits of these successful firms, when ploughed back into expansion, generate large-scale employment of skilled workers, and the incomes earned by them strengthen the demand for goods and services which these very firms are producing cost effectively. Thus, in a competitive economy, improved supplies (through lower costs) meet increased demand (through larger employment and income) and the economy is put on the path of economic growth.

This is how the West European and the North American economies reached their present position where the costs of production of output are so low in relation to enhanced incomes that masses of the previously poor populations have all come to benefit from the low-cost, low-priced and highly efficient consumer goods including durable consumer goods of a wide variety. It is in this manner that poverty diminished enormously in the first world and such symptoms are now emerging in the third world as a result of structural reforms and the aforementioned processes. It is only when these steps are taken in other developing countries that mass access of the population to numerous goods and service will occur and trends will be set in motion for poverty reduction.

After the firms that could not compete nor merge with others go out of business, as they will, the firms that remain in business will be those that could compete effectively with the West European, North American and Pacific region enterprises. As goods and services of mass consumption become available at low and affordable prices, the stage would be set for the reduction and elimination of poverty in countries which are now in the process of structural adjustment. However, it should be pointed out, in warning, that the route described above is not the only route and that there is 'many a slip between cup and lip'. The market economy has its negative aspects as well as positive ones, in that monopolies and oligopolies are also a part of the market economy and, if allowed to survive noncompetitively, would be seen to be full of negative results in respect of growth and poverty annihilation. There is also the problem of recurring recessions which detract from a smooth trend of growth and development and make poverty raise its ugly head again and again.

15 Strategies for Poverty Reduction in Different Regimes

Nearly all politico-economic regimes in the nineteenth and the twentieth centuries have had the issues of economic growth, income redistribution and poverty reduction built into their economic philosophies, either explicitly or implicitly.

THE LAISSEZ-FAIRE REGIME

Being based essentially on laissez-faire individualism, Adam Smith's free-market approach did not have a specifically defined strategy for poverty reduction; but poverty reduction was seen implicitly as the end-product which would finally emerge as a result of the interactions of demand and supply. The market economies of Western Europe and North America, Japan, Australia and New Zealand, in the twentieth century, despite new advances of thought, have had the underpinnings of Adam Smith's economic philosophy in their thought-patterns and economic organization. Their belief is that in a competitive environment, with the release of market forces and the urge to expand through competition, which keeps prices low, profits normal and technologies improving all the time, the final result would be the greatest good of the greatest number. This market strategy did not rule out the existence nor the emergence of unemployment from time to time especially during the down-swing and recessionary phases of the trade cycle. But it was asserted that in such situations competition among the workers would lead to a decline in wages and lower wage rates would then enhance employment once again, until full employment is reached – and poverty reduction would be a function of employment. The many 'ifs' and 'buts' in reaching the stage of full employment and poverty reduction were of course noted and debated but it was hoped that eventually this stage would be reached. Among the 'ifs' and 'buts', the existence of monopoly and oligopoly (the domination of one firm or a few firms in the market for any given product) was also seen as a detracting feature which compromises competition and prevents the benefits of the market economy from reaching the poor. But even monopoly and oligopoly, it was hoped, would melt away as the competitive forces took over in the long run.

155

Essentially, the philosophy and the organization of the market economy stood on strong logical ground in asserting that ultimately unemployment and poverty would disappear. Even though this did not actually happen, great strides were taken in the market system towards the promotion of phenomenal economic growth, which involved the working classes in rising employment and eventually gave them periodic full employment. Later on, in the twentieth century, through strong social and political pressures, social services for health, education and unemployment compensation were installed in the market economies. And still later, the populations of the market-oriented societies came to have the benefits of mass-produced and affordable consumer goods and services.

The market economies of North America, Europe, Japan, Australia and New Zealand – in short, the first world – witnessed the coexistence of urbanization, commercialization, industrialization and agricultural transformation in the nineteenth and early twentieth centuries and had the advantage of technological and communications revolutions, somewhat later in the twentieth century. As the economic philosophy of the market place coexisted with these great revolutions, it is debatable whether the forces of the market economy caused and promoted the revolutions or the revolutions strengthened the practice of the market economy. Be that as it may, it is clear that the market economy and the revolutions taken together did impact poverty in a substantial measure. Nevertheless, poverty could not be totally conquered and the phenomenon of recessions and recoveries – lean years followed by fat years – remained a fact of economic life.

The logical foundation for the belief that poverty would eventually be eliminated in the market economy was fascinating and quite persuasive. After all, the consumers, being sovereign and not obstructed by controls and restrictions, would exercise their preferences and would demand different goods in different quantities depending upon their tastes, their income levels and the relative prices of the products in question. As the consumers asserted their demand preferences and shifted from one product to another or one substitute to another, the price of the preferred products would rise. Then the suppliers, seeking their profits and in competition with each other, would begin to shift from other products to the preferred products and would produce more of the latter. In that case, the additional supplies would annihilate the additional demands and the price of the preferred products would fall back to normal once again. During the phase of rising prices of the preferred product, profits of the producers of that product would increase; but as more producers shift into this product and compete for sales, profits would fall back to normal, owing to a price decline. Thus, prices and profits would tend to reach some normal levels again and extraordinary profits would not survive for long.

During the phase of rising prices and profits of one or many products, the producers or suppliers would employ more resources of labour, capital and technology in those products. As more labour would be demanded in this phase of price and profit increase, a larger number of workers would offer their services and might even train themselves in the production of the preferred products. With rising profitability, the producers too would offer higher wages to tempt the workers from unpreferred to preferred lines and also tempt the unemployed to join the employment stream. Thus, with a larger supply of labour, and consequently with a larger supply of the preferred products, as the product prices fell back to normal, higher wages too would be converted into lower wages and a kind of normal wage rate would begin to prevail once again.

Similarly, in a competitive situation, as the producers order more resources in the preferred products and employ a larger capital stock, some entrepreneurs and technologists would invent new technology and thus enrich the quality of capital as well as labour. Innovativeness in a competitive economy would thus be an important characteristic so that the market economy could be credited with a high degree of inventiveness and a large number of innovations. The basic point is that the market economy would bring innovation, scale economies and profitability on the one side and increased employment and income on the other. Making effective supply and effective demand move hand in hand, it would promote economic growth and thus result in the greatest good of the greatest number. Hence, a positive dent would be made in poverty.

All this, however, did not happen everywhere in the market economies; but what actually happened over a century and a half or more was impressive enough in terms of promoting economic growth, greater levels of employment and inventiveness. The market economy could also be credited with a fundamental characteristic, namely the absence of a dictator in organizing the economic system and directing it according to his own arbitrary will. Such autocratic handling and economic dictation could either be effective or preposterously faulty, inefficient and unproductive. On the other hand, in the market economy, as Adam Smith asserted, the invisible hand of nature would guide the system and would bring about, without arbitrariness, the greatest good of the greatest number. As stated, the system worked and brought immense benefits especially aided and abetted by industrial, agricultural, commercial and technological revolutions and put mass-produced and cost-effective goods and services into the hands of the poor as well as the rich. Nevertheless, at the end of a century and a half of its working, the market-oriented world remained a poor place and even the market economies with their recessions and fluctuations, did not really conquer the problem of poverty.

To any analyst of mass poverty, two lessons ring out loud and clear from the experience of the nineteenth and the twentieth centuries. The first is that the unstructured approach of the market economy, which allows free play to the forces of demand and supply under the 'invisible hand of nature', even without any particular policy for poverty reduction, has an important causal connection with the economic uplift of the masses and a substantial reduction in poverty. In countries and regions in which the free market prescription was practised consistently, economic revolutions have, in fact, occurred; and aided and abetted by these revolutions – primarily the industrial, agricultural, commercial, transport, communications and information revolutions – the populations of the first world have experienced a phenomenal reduction in poverty. For a future onslaught on the remaining poverty in these regions, the basic tenets of the market economy and the forces of liberalization are essential policy ingredients and should be continued – albeit with some major qualifications and additional policies.

The second lesson from historical experience is that the market economy is a necessary but not a sufficient mechanism for a total elimination of poverty. In other words, the market economy has to be tempered by some other prescriptions inasmuch as the existence and recurrence of the trade cycle, with its depressions and recoveries, its downturns and upturns, detracts from the growth trend of the market economies and causes poverty to recur periodically, making millions of people move from prosperity to adversity and perhaps back to prosperity again. Moreover, since the market economy, as Adam Smith also noted, is not just a competitive economy but also contains monopolistic and oligopolistic structures, poverty never melts away totally. This factor, together with recurring depressions in the past and recurring recessions in the present times, makes poverty persist and does not guarantee either full employment or a continuous improvement in public welfare. That is why anti-cyclical policies, periodic shifts from balanced budgets to deficit budgets, launching of public works programmes and the installation of safety nets in the shape of social services, have had to be launched as a necessary adjunct to the continuation of the market economy, if poverty is to be contained.

THE WELFARE STATE

The welfare state took root in Western Europe only in the post-World War II period but was clearly practised as an answer to the negative aspects of the market economy. Nevertheless, the welfare state did not invalidate the market economy but modified it here and there and provided for interventions in all the major European economies. Its political counterpart often went in the name of democratic socialism or social democracy and, in any case, sought to provide cushions to the working class and the middle class against the evils of depressions and inflation. This phase in the market economies did result in a redistribution of income in favour of the blue-collared and white-collared workers and modified some of the extreme situations in terms of towering heights of prosperity on the one side and disturbing depths of depression on the other.

After some decades of the operation of the welfare state in Europe and the USA, it became clear that this organization suffered from two handicaps. The welfare state involved huge subsidies in food, education, health services and housing and the running of some key infrastructures used by the general public such as electric power and transportation. Subsidized goods and services have the habit of proliferating from essentials to non-essentials and from target to non-target groups. Subsidies also cause excess demand and can be greatly abused. Subsidies, like price controls, initially provided with the best of intentions, become political and, once provided, cannot be lessened or abolished. Moreover, the subsidized welfare services, in due course, become a burden on the state exchequer and as they cannot be sustained, policy tussles emerge on how to reduce or remove them. All this happened to many a welfare state, and as some services came to naught and others ran inefficiently, the impact on poverty was not as great as expected – and poverty persisted in many countries, although perhaps in reduced form. Thus the welfare state is a mechanism seemingly opposite to the market economy but actually turns out to be an adjunct to it, as it has evolved in the twentieth century, especially in the market economies, and later, spread to some others as well.

With the march of democracy in the industrialized economies, often termed the first world, the recurrence of the trade cycle, the emergence and re-emergence of massive unemployment, the periodic declines and increases in prices and the persistence as well as periodic recurrence of poverty became a matter of public conscience and could not be tolerated. Intellectual and practical inputs were bestowed on these issues in the first half of the twentieth century, particularly after World Wars I and II, and the welfare state came to be evolved. The welfare state did not set aside the basic characteristics of the market economy but only superimposed on it, with different degrees of policy interventions and innovations, some new mechanisms for the control of the trade cycle, the reduction of unemployment and a substantial reduction in poverty.

The New Deal in the United States during the regime of President Roosevelt, in the period after the Great Depression (1929–33) and thereafter, gave a new turn to the market economy. Budget deficits in order to promote public expenditures on public works, welfare services and unemployment benefits came to be accepted. Support for the idea of strong trade unions to negotiate with the governments for the protection of the working class also came to be justified and then prevailed in all market economies. Economic recovery from the Great Depression remained weak, and depressed economies, with continuing collapse and liquidation of industrial and commercial firms and banking crises sometimes leading to closures, continued in the inter-war period, both in the USA and Western Europe.

The success of the market economies in raising the standard of living of millions of the poor – though not of all of them – was undeniable, but equally undeniable was the poverty and misery of the remaining poor whose numbers also ran into millions, at any rate during the depths of depressions. As discussed earlier, the latter phenomenon of persisting poverty and increasing misery had two quite different outcomes in two different parts of the world in the first half of the twentieth century. One was the emergence of the welfare state in North America, Western Europe and some other market economies, and the other was the Communist Revolution and the launching of a planned economy, which later spread to the countries of Eastern Europe, generally seen as satellites of the Soviet Union.

THE PLANNED ECONOMIES AND THE COMMUNIST STATE

The leaders of communist thought, from Marx and Engels to Lenin and Stalin, regarded the unequal distribution of income and wealth, the recurrence of the trade cycle and the misery of the working classes (the proletariat) as built-in characteristics of the capitalist economy. They came up with strong theoretical formulations against the capitalist state and many practical propositions to overthrow it with the force of a proletarian revolution. The communist movement succeeded in overthrowing the Czarist regime in Russia, and, later on, somewhat similar autocratic regimes in Eastern Europe, and set up several communist states. A key objective of the Communist Revolution was the institution of the planned economy, in which, alongside aggressive capital formation, central planning, state enterprises, collective farms and state farms came to be the instruments of state policy. These were to be used for the annihilation of poverty, the removal of the trade cycle, the provision of high employment, near-equality in the distribution of income and wealth through taxes and subsidies, and the provision of housing, health measures and educational establish-ments. Techniques of planning were evolved and emphasis came to be put on the management of demand, control of consumption and an attempt to augment saving, both personal and institutional, essentially through heavy taxation – all of which were to be strictly implemented.

A succession of Five Year Plans for economic development, the aboli-tion of private property, the organization of industry by central decision making and the direction of labour, the setting up of collective and state farms and the prohibition of private trade, rents and profits and of private employment of man by man, were some of the key characteristics of the communist economic organization. Despite the aftermath of a bloody revo-lution and all the strictness and arbitrariness of decision making carried out by an economic oligarchy, the planned economies could, nevertheless, be credited with huge capital formation, increase in output, increase in employment, improved distribution of income and wealth and substantial reduction in poverty. However, the lack of freedom of enterprise, an absence of the incentive of private property and the exploitation inherent in an autocratic economic system detracted greatly from public welfare and modified the effectiveness of the economic system, not to mention the miseries caused by a non-accountable political regime which was respon-sible for many an injustice and inequity.

Before, and even after, the end of the Stalinist era in the early 1950s, the organization of the communist state revealed numerous intolerable fea-tures of the physically planned economies and unjust policies. In the 1960s and 1970s, the system began its first moves towards semi-liberalization. Workers in the collective farms were allotted small plots of land within the collectives with some freedom to generate their own agricultural produce and sell it in newly established market places. In these markets, govern-ment officials and statisticians collected data on the state of demand for and supply of different commodities, and the movement of prices. These price movements were noted and became important inputs in the next time period for the allocation of resources in different commodities in order to bring commodity-wise production in line with demands expressed not only in these markets but also in the price-and-quantity-controlled ones. Suppose the management of collective farms had allocated 1000 units of resources in wheat production and only 800 units in beef production. If the market situation noted by government statisticians showed a fall in price and accumulation of stocks in wheat – underlining a shortage of demand in relation to supply – and if prices showed a rise of demand in the beef market with the lengthening of the queues in that market – exhibiting an excess demand in relation to supply – the management of the collective farms revised their allocations and shifted resources from wheat to beef. In that case, in the next time period, as beef supplies increased and wheat supplies were reduced, beef prices would go down in the market and wheat prices would rise to normal levels. Thus, with one intervention by the government statisticians and collective farm management, the laws of demand and supply came to be respected somewhat more and the first moves were in sight towards a market-oriented economy.

Meanwhile, the Soviet and the East European economies did make it the state's responsibility to provide housing for the whole population. Housing space was never sufficient and the quality was generally unimpressive. But it is true that nearly everyone had a roof over his or her head, though congestion prevailed and low-quality housing had to be tolerated by the citizens.

It is also true that by the early 1970s, income distribution in the Soviet Union had become impressively equitable. In general, the lowest paid worker, say a janitor woman, would get around 60 roubles per month while the highest paid functionary would have about 600 roubles, not to mention a few thousand privileged citizens such as politicians, higher bureaucrats, top scientists and cosmonauts who could get 1500 roubles per month. If a husband and wife were both scientists of some calibre they could enjoy a really comfortable income and more elaborate housing space and live in a kind of luxury. But others had to put up with poorer housing.

In the Soviet Union, no man could employ another man and no man could run an industrial or commercial business and make a profit out of it; no one could indulge in foreign trade and no one could pay rents to anyone officially. One could, no doubt, save out of one's income and put the saving in a bank account, which would earn about 3 per cent interest per annum. But one could not have more than one house nor a house be rented out for earnings. Citizens of working age in the Soviet Union and East European countries would be given employment and nearly every one of them, except those in transition, could be said to be employed. But closer investigation showed millions of them to be ineffectively employed or under-employed, producing very little or, in any case, well below their full employment capacity.

Thus, in many senses despite low productivity and serious inefficiencies, the Soviet and the East European system of the planned economy cushioned the poor a great deal, provided a semblance of full employment, poor quality housing (barring exceptions), and access to essential consumer goods (though not always adequate in terms of quantity and quality). But the good intentions of the system were marred by bureaucratic inefficiencies, shortages, illicit dealings, restrictions of all sorts and a lack of incentives and motivation.

The inadequacies and the stresses of the system finally began to tell. When the political forces generated during the regime of Mr Gorbachev seriously questioned the huge machinery of nuclear and non-nuclear armament building, the existence of stressful bureaucracy and the inefficiency of the economic mechanism, the system began to collapse and subsequently gave way completely within a short period. There was a bid to return to the free market system in which private enterprises would be permitted, ownership of property and capital formation by private individuals and firms would be allowed and the forces of demand and supply could begin to work. But the period of transition since the end of the Gorbachev days, the break up of the Soviet Union and the establishment of independent republics tied together in a Confederation of Independent States (CIS), has been extremely painful and continues to be so today. The communist state has withered away in all the republics, the planned economy seems to be in tatters, the command economy and the controlled regime have collapsed but the return to the market economy is not coming easily. In the last 70 years or so, millions of people seem to have lost touch with the handling of market forces and, in any case, the building up of new private enterprises, with adequate provision of capital stock, infrastructures, advanced technologies, trained managers and efficient labour force, is very much at a discount, given USSR's history. The system today is in a state of flux, struggling to return from the command economy to the market economy, and meanwhile, by all accounts, poverty has surfaced and seems to be on the increase, as earlier chapters have shown.

THE MIXED ECONOMY APPROACH TO POVERTY REDUCTION

Dissatisfied with the performance of the market economy in the nineteenth and the early twentieth centuries and observing the persistence of poverty, while countries of the first world began to practise various forms of the welfare state, and the Soviet Union and the East European countries adopted a rigorously planned economy, a large number of developing countries in Asia, Latin America and Africa were seized by the problem of growth, development and poverty reduction and adopted the mixed economy model in the second half of the twentieth century. This consisted largely of allowing the markets to function normally in many sectors and sub-sectors while practising market interventions in other sectors in different ways and in varying degrees. Borrowing some aspects of economic planning from the Soviet experience, many developing economies adopted economic planning models and allied policies which basically emphasized high capital formation, rapid industrial and agricultural growth and serious attention to income redistribution and poverty reduction. The concept of the poverty line was evolved and policies were focused on lifting up the masses from below the poverty line to a position above it. The poverty line, below which the population was deemed to be poor, varied from country to country and within a country from time to time.

The institution of a Planning Commission in many cases, the operation of government-sponsored industries in the public sector, the construction of basic infrastructures such as electric power, road transportation, production of steel and non-ferrous metals, mining ventures and irrigation projects and fertilizer plants to strengthen the agricultural sector and to produce abundant food and raw material, were common features of the planning strategies. Investment was encouraged, both in the public and the private sectors in these mixed economies but the construction of basic infrastructures in projects which had large forward and backward linkages was designed to work in the public sector of enterprise. Measures for literacy, education and health improvement also remained generally the responsibility of the government, though private organizations were also allowed to work in these areas.

While all these efforts had an indirect, and some a direct, impact on poverty reduction, the basic methods for poverty reduction, practised with different degrees of success, were an attempt at inflation control which affected the masses favourably, and the operation of many specific programmes of economic development and poverty reduction. In those developing economies, particularly in the Far East, such as Korea, Taiwan and the ASEAN countries, wittily nicknamed the 'Asian Tigers', which accepted a larger market orientation, the operation of development programmes and anti-poverty programmes was not so common. As the growth rates of these economies in the second half of the twentieth century were in the region of 6 to 10 per cent per annum and population growth was around 3 per cent per annum, the per capita growth was seen to be between 3 and 7 per cent. That kind of growth obviously trickled down and involved the poorer populations in economic activity. This made a dent in poverty. But in the general run of the developing mixed economies, which depended on planned development and had a slower growth rate such as 3–4 per cent per year and a population growth between 2 and 3 per cent a net per capita growth between 1 and 2 per cent – turned out to be insufficient for the trickle-down effect. In the absence of a trickle down, the mass of the population was seen to be uninvolved generally in the growth process and, therefore, various programmes of development and uplift from poverty were designed in the hope that if growth did not bring the people out of poverty, the

programmes would. Thus, a country like India ran a large number of pro-
grammes such as the Community Development Programme (CDP), the
Backward Area Development Programme, the Primary Health Centres and
Sub-Centres and others.

In many of these countries, as a result of such efforts, poverty was reduced
either overall or in particular sectors and segments. The process of industrialization, the rise in agricultural productivity – thanks to the green
(agricultural) revolution in several countries, greater opportunities for
employment and greater attention to educational and health measures, did
cause an improvement in economic levels and lifted up the poor in most
developing countries. In some countries the control of inflation also
helped the poor and the rich alike. The programmes mentioned above and
others similar to these were effective in many cases. These programmes,
however, had two features which detracted from their full and wholesome
impact. One was the corrupt practices which often emerge in such programmes, filling the pockets of intermediaries and government officials,
with the result that the benefits do not reach the poor in the desired volumes and values. The late Professor Raj Krishna once joked about India's
beneficiary-oriented programmes: 'At one time some benefits were leak-
ing out to the officials and the intermediaries; but now the officials are getting the benefits and the beneficiaries are only getting the leak!'

The other feature was the lack of incentive and the inherent inefficiency
characteristic of these programmes. With regard to public sector programmes
in education and health, it has often been observed that the newly established village schools suffer from absenteeism among the teachers and lack
of basic facilities such as blackboards, textbooks and notebooks. The absenteeism of doctors and nurses and thousands of unfilled posts of these func-
tionaries together with the shortage of medicines on the shelves of clinics
and health centres also tells a sorry tale. This, however, is not to deny that
in countries like India, some benefits have in fact been received by the poor
so much so that the population below the poverty line has declined from
48 to 39 per cent and, by some reckoning, to 31 per cent and even 18 per
cent in the late 1980s and the early 1990s. Debate continues on the correct-
ness of these figures but even so a reduction of the poverty proportion cannot be denied.

This, however, does not mean a reduction in the absolute number of the
poor. The general picture is that while the absolute number of the poor has
been increasing, the non-poor are increasing in larger numbers. In a case
like India, in the 1990s, the absolute number of the poor has also begun to
decline and segmental poverty, such as literacy and educational poverty,
health poverty, food poverty and income poverty, has begun to show a

reduction. The Human Development Index for many developing countries has been showing an improvement even though the pace of improvement is extremely slow.

The moral seems to be that while development programmes and anti-poverty programmes in developing mixed economies practising some semblance of economic planning do result in some decline in poverty, the main vehicle for poverty reduction, as in the market-oriented developing economies, is rapid economic growth and a decline in inflation rates. The mixed economies do not seem to have achieved any glowing success in these two respects through the anti-poverty programmes. But in the case of the market-oriented developing countries like South Korea and the ASEAN, it was the release of the market forces and the productive energies of the people, that seem to have led to the establishment of a 6–10 per cent annual growth which was a major cause of poverty reduction. Not so in the remaining developing economies which had only sporadic success in poverty reduction.

STRUCTURAL REFORMS AND A RETURN TO THE MARKET ECONOMIES WITH A DIFFERENCE

Exasperated by the slowness of economic development and poverty reduction and facing a series of economic crises, a large number of developing countries have launched a process of structural reforms in the late 1980s and the first half of the 1990s. These reforms have many dimensions but they invariably include a reduction of price, investment, foreign-exchange, import and export controls and many other restrictions, in particular, the licensing, rationing and quota systems. These reforms envisage a reduction in subsidies and government expenditures, a cut in budget deficits and fiscal deficits as a proportion of the GDP and a reduction of tax rates, both direct and indirect. The focus of the reforms is on a contraction of the public sector of enterprise and an expansion of private sector activity, with freedom to undertake investment activity unhindered by licences and permits. In external relations, the structural reforms provide for a freer flow of foreign capital, the determination of the foreign exchange rate of local currencies through the market forces of demand and supply, rather than an official *fiat* from the Central Banks and the Ministries of Finance, and a substitution of export-generation strategies in place of import substitution. These reforms have worked with different degrees of success in different developing countries in the last few years, but the process is still incomplete inasmuch as the structural changes have remained confined to a few functional areas and sectors and still leave the liberalization and deregulation of many sectors to the future.

Though the reforms generally do not speak explicitly of poverty reduction, it is clear that there is a major strategy for poverty reduction implicit in the structural reform process. This consists of policies for the elimination of the monopoly of one firm, or the oligopoly of a few firms, by providing entry without cumbersome licensing procedures to many competitive firms in each line and thus allowing competition to take its own course. Competition, it is expected, would put pressure on the inefficient firms and either lead to their closure or a merger or amalgamation with other more efficient firms which would take over the inefficient ones. The firms which survive in the competitive era, would have greater efficiency and lower costs per unit of output. They would also have enlarged scales of production and economies of scale and access to new technologies and better management. The fact that they would be working in a competitive and non-oligopolistic environment would guarantee their efficiency and profitability and, in due course, enable them to generate mass-produced goods and services. As the scales of production widen and profits are ploughed back, employment would increase too and larger incomes would be the necessary outcome. With large wage incomes (as well as profit incomes) on the demand side and large volumes of mass-produced goods on the supply side, the poor would begin to have access to efficient goods and services in large numbers and would be released from poverty in due course.

16 Package of Policies for Poverty Elimination

What do we learn from the half-dozen regimes we have examined about the success and failure of policies and practices for poverty reduction? Combing through the successful and unsuccessful efforts in these regimes, spanning about two centuries, what package of policies and practices can we develop for eliminating the huge volume of poverty that still remains in all categories of nations we have studied and threatens to increase further in some categories or countries?

LAISSEZ-FAIRE

From the great breakthrough achieved by Adam Smith with his advocacy of the free market economy, and its adoption by many countries in Western Europe and North America in the nineteenth century, we see that despite many limitations and failures, the economic face of Western Europe and North America altered beyond recognition, economic growth took over from stagnation and numerous avenues opened up for the poor to obtain gainful employment and get out of poverty. This leads us to the prime recommendation for **the adoption of the market economy, where it does not exist, and its strengthening, where it does exist,** as this is a basic condition for growth, employment expansion and poverty reduction. This involves the removal of interventions, interferences and over-regulations which detract from the free operation of the forces of demand and supply, as far and as fast as possible.

Observation of the economic and social phenomena in the eighteenth and nineteenth centuries makes it clear that the expansion of the market economy in Western Europe and North America coexisted with the unfolding of the great economic revolutions – urban, commercial, agricultural and industrial. It is debatable whether the market economy propelled the great revolutions or whether the revolutions gave an impetus to the market economy. However, the coexistence of the two path-breaking occurrences is undeniable and it is also very probable that the two phenomena were mutually reinforcing.

The combined effects of the revolutions, aided and abetted by the market economy, and vice versa, have certainly revolutionized the West

European and the North American scene and brought about a surge of affluence on the one hand and a decline in poverty on the other. This is another compelling reason why present and future efforts to reduce or eliminate poverty should not fail to move in the direction of introducing and strengthening market forces, as this is one prime way to cause the great revolutions in regimes in which these have not yet arrived. Poverty reduction is a certainty when the commercial, agricultural and industrial revolutions occur and the strengthening of the market economy does seem to be a significant cause of these occurrences.

This, however, is not a prescription for a 'laissez-fairy' land in which the unbridled competition of everybody with everybody else is supposed to add up somehow to the greatest good of the greatest number. The market economy in the late twentieth and twenty-first centuries should not be understood to stand for the law of the jungle in which the poor, the weak and the sick are abandoned and pushed to the wall. Actually, the market economy, as it exits in many places today, has several negative and unproductive features. Some of these have to be removed by governmental or societal action and some have to be monitored and directed by professional bodies and social groups into constructive channels. It is not true that a market economy does not have or need any controls and regulations. Controls are needed to check malpractices and deviations but these do not have to be exercised only by the government – they can also be exercised by acknowledged and designated professional and technical authorities and bodies and to some extent by governmental organizations and non-government organizations (NGOs).

It is also noteworthy that the market economy we laud as a saviour, is a healthy and competitive economy, free from monopolies, oligopolies and the Mafia. But the market economy of today, even in advanced industrial countries, is not always a scene of perfect or fair competition, as it includes monopolistic firms (a single supplier of a given product) and oligopolistic firms (a few market-dominant corporations producing a particular product). Such firms which detract from competition aim at restricting production, colluding with each other to keep prices high, influencing the governments through unfair means, indulging in malpractices and fleecing the consumers. This is the reason why many countries like the USA, UK and Germany found it necessary to pass anti-monopoly laws and set up commissions and consumer protection organizations to implement them. Thus the next recommendation that is necessary in the context of a well-performing market economy is **to evolve legislation and practices for the elimination of monopoly and oligopoly, allow freedom of entry into various lines of production, and set up professional and expert**

institutions for monitoring public and private enterprises, preventing deviations and malpractices and protecting consumer interest.

It is, of course, true that Adam Smith's laissez-faire had an enormous impact on Western Europe and North America, gave impetus to the great revolutions, fostered a shift from stagnation to growth and brought millions of the poor into gainful employment, income growth and poverty reduction. But laissez-faire did not have an explicit strategy for poverty elimination and such end-products in terms of poverty reduction which it might have implied were too long-term and distant. Laissez-faire was more oriented towards physical capital resource but it neglected human resource development and had no strategy for its enhancement either. In other words, the great social services in education, health, housing and employment were neglected. Even more importantly, in the laissez-faire philosophy, the phenomenon of the trade cycle or business cycle kept making people poor from time to time – in depressions and recessions – and this cyclical poverty detracted substantially from sustained secular trend growth. Thus, economic growth under laissez-faire was not sustainable.

We also note that though the rest of the world outside Western Europe and North America had a kind of crude market economy, Adam Smith's refinements did not touch that world. At the end of 100 to 150 years of laissez-faire, three-quarters of the world's population stayed poor. On the whole, it can be observed that age-old poverty persisted in the under-developed countries and poverty with a difference remained a feature of the laissez-faire type of market economies at the beginning of the twentieth century. In the first half of the twentieth century, two major, and entirely different, approaches to the conquest of poverty emerged – the welfare state and the communist state – and these were followed in the second half by yet another approach to economic growth and poverty reduction adopted by the under-developed, non-industrial economies of the world. This was the mixed economy approach.

THE SOCIALIST ANSWER TO THE POVERTY PHENOMENON

Despite the colossal negative features of bloody revolutions and dictatorships, the communist state did emphasize income redistribution, employment generation, housing, health facilities, educational facilities and other social benefits to reduce and eliminate poverty. One of the noteworthy positive features of the Soviet and East European command economies was the *will* to install social services and reduce poverty. These services did go a considerable distance towards eradicating poverty, and provided employment and housing for all and health and educational facilities for nearly everybody. However, there remained a great deal of concealed unemployment or under-employment and housing remained of poor quality and congested. The direction of labour, the bureaucratic allocation of capital, hand-picking of managers from below and imposition from above in industry and in agricultural collective and state farms left the economy without incentives – a huge monolith of an economic machine which moved sluggishly and did not generate enough goods and services either in quantity or quality to match the (suppressed) demand. The system did not respect the price mechanism and did not provide support for the sustainability, continuation and expansion of the great social programmes of income distribution, employment generation, housing, health and education. At the end of the day, these programmes which were to play a key role in poverty reduction were cut to the bone and became unsustainable as they could not receive resource support from the productive mechanism of a command economy. What has to be picked up as a recommendation from the socialist experiment for a universal effort for poverty reduction is **the will of the state – to which has to be added the will of the society – to launch programmes of sustainable literacy, education, health, housing and employment.** Some of the details of the techniques which are used to put the will of the state into practice may also be borrowed from the Soviet and East European experiment, but others have to be shunned and avoided, particularly the colossal intervention and interference of political dictatorship and rigid bureaucracy. Accountable institutions and professional bodies – rather than governments and officialdom – have to manage these great objectives and programmes for growth of poverty elimination.

THE WELFARE STATE AND ATTEMPTS TO FIGHT POVERTY

Outside the fold of the communist state, the alternative answer to the continued prevalence of poverty was the welfare state in the democratic regimes of the twentieth century. The welfare state provided just that missing link in the laissez-faire set-up which could sustain the market economy and avoid the serious criticism that the market economy was inhuman, violently fluctuating and unmindful of poverty. The missing link in the laissez-faire economy recently provided by the welfare state was the provision of social services and safety nets in terms of education, health and medical facilities, unemployment compensation, social insurance, maternity benefits, old age pensions and the like. These are the pioneering and innovative contributions of the welfare state which could be picked up and made an integral part of the present and future strategy of all countries for the elimination of poverty. That these great social service programmes receive support and acclaim from the people – who are the beneficiaries – makes them sustainable in a democracy, provided that economic resources do not go short and destroy the programmes. What sustained the welfare state and its crucial programmes – in the USA, Canada, Western Europe, Japan, Australia and New Zealand – was the acceptance, by and large, of the market economy rather than the command economy.

In other words, the welfare state accepted one aspect of the socialist prescriptions and rejected the other: it accepted the programmes of social benefits but rejected the communist revolution, the dictatorship of the pro-letariat and the command economy. It is clear that the continuation and acceptance of the market economy, with its growth potential, enabled the welfare state to provide sustenance to the great social services and work effectively towards poverty reduction and elimination. Thus, if any part of the future strategy of poverty reduction in democratic countries is to be borrowed from the welfare state and made into a recommendation, it is **the provision of sustainable social services for literacy, education, health, medicine, housing, employment and various arrangements for unem-ployment compensation, social insurance, old age pensions, maternity benefits and similar social provisions with some user-cost payments.**

As the periodic occurrence of recessions has not been conquered by the market economies, even in the welfare states, and unemployment has assumed menacing proportions – 6–7 per cent of workforce in the USA (seven million people) and 9 per cent in Germany (four million people) in the mid-1990s – it is the **adoption of counter-cyclical fiscal policies, timely adjustment of monetary and interest rate policies, well-timed programmes for housing and infrastructural build-up – together with the provision of social services, unemployment compensation and social insurance – that can provide a cushion against recurring poverty.**

Somewhere on its way to poverty abolition, the welfare state began to lose its way as it adopted policies and prescriptions which did not really promote welfare, economic growth and poverty reduction but actually began to detract from these objectives. Even as it borrowed the correct ideas from the Soviet Union, in the shape of an emphasis on social safety nets, it also borrowed what would appear to be the wrong ideas in the shape of state-run industries, price controls, quantitative restrictions and direction of labour. The social services began to take on a populist charac-ter with a promise to provide free services. The welfare state, beginning with President Roosevelt's New Deal in the United States and followed by almost every government in Western Europe, began to legitimize huge governmental expenditures and colossal budget deficits without asking users of social services – at any rate those who could afford them – to pay for these services. Soon the welfare state was involved in unsustainable deficit spending, inefficient social services and loss-making industries. However, correctives seem to have been applied quite early and one by one, in the post-World War II era, moves were made to get rid of the untenable deviations. The trend towards the nationalization of industries slowed down and was given up later, as in the case of countries such as the UK where Thatcherism, with its emphasis on privatization, took over.

From the experience of the welfare state, a series of measures can be recommended to help a future onslaught on poverty. **Price controls have to be replaced by free markets, and quantitative restrictions, such as rationing and quotas, by market-oriented quantities ordered by demand and supply. The direction of labour must be given up, health services should begin to charge the users a price linked with their paying capacity, and the market orientation of costs and prices must become the order of the day once again.** Moreover, the great lesson that has to be learned from the welfare states of Western Europe, North America and Australia is **the development of a will on the part of the state to launch those major social services, back them up through the provision of resources, implement them rigorously, give up the loss-making as well as the non-sustainable nationalized industries and allow the market mechanism to provide efficient resources to industry and trade as well as to governments so as to have enough wherewithal to support the social safety network.**

THE MIXED ECONOMIES WITH A MIX OF ECONOMIC PLANNING AND THE MARKET MECHANISM

The awakening of under-developed countries (politely known as the developing economies) to their own poverty and to a burning desire to overcome it, dates from the period after World War II in the middle of the twentieth century. Around this time, these countries began to be aware of and to respond to theories of economic growth and economic planning. Their basic intention was to achieve the objectives of rapid economic growth of output and income, bring about a redistribution of the consequent rising incomes in favour of the poor, make income growth possible through capital formation out of domestic saving as well as foreign saving, and endeavour to generate as much employment as possible with a view to poverty reduction. To meet these objectives, the crucial instrument of progress was to be a growth in saving and investment, including foreign saving, together with an improvement in the efficiency of capital use (by a decline in capital-output ratio), a slow-down in population growth and some provision of social services. The developing countries were greatly influenced by the socialist planning models though they had a softer formulation of the model with fewer rigidities and with the prevalence of the market mechanism, except in respect of some goods and services where controls and interventions were felt to be desirable.

To cut a long story short, these semi-planned economies of the developing nations did show some progress in terms of achieving higher growth rates, larger capital formation, larger employment and some marginal redistribution of income through the mechanism of taxes and subsidies. But the experience of 40 years, from 1951 to 1991, began to show that while achieving a higher growth rate – say, around 5 per cent per year – these economies became bogged down in bureaucratic rigidities, budget deficits, inefficiencies and high capital-output ratios, especially in the public sector of enterprise, inefficient capital formation in agriculture, disincentives for work and savings and, eventually, a slow-down in the growth rate itself. Many of these economies became the scene of one crisis after another. For instance, between 1989–91, the Indian economy was gripped by three crises – a crisis of budgetary shortages making the construction of infrastructure virtually impossible and the running of anti-poverty programmes difficult; a crisis in balance of payments and foreign exchange; and a crisis of production and supplies with numerous brakes and restrictions on capacity building and output growth.

Structural Adjustment Programmes

In the light of these experiences, the developing economies began to give up the planning approach and the mixed pattern and shifted to what are called structural adjustment programmes. The major recommendations in the structural adjustment process are: **a denationalization of industries, a move towards privatization, the establishment of new industries only in the private sector, a cut in the tax rates** with a view to collecting larger tax revenues through larger turnovers and higher income, **a reduction in government expenditures, a cut in budget deficits and fiscal deficits in relation to GDP, a reduction in inflation rates as well as interest rates** (for larger capital formation), **the determination of the foreign exchange rate of the local currency through the forces of demand and supply in the market place** rather than by administrative *fiat* from the Central Banks and the Ministries of Finance, **a freer flow of foreign capital, greater acquisition of new technologies from abroad, a switch from import substitution to export generation** – and, in general, **a shift towards a market-oriented liberalized economy and an open and so-called globalized economy.**

These measures of structural reform, which are replacing the over-controlled and over-regulated semi-planned and mixed economies, are still unfolding in the developing nations, and much is expected of them in the way of faster growth rates, higher efficiency, larger resource generation in terms of saving and investment, higher employment and a considerable reduction in poverty. The chances are that, in general, in most of these countries, the aforementioned measures will succeed. Meanwhile, by pruning the history of the recent 50 years in the developing semi-planned market economies, the following can be recommended. If the eventual elimination of poverty is the aim, policy makers must note that:

- A great deal of respect for the forces of demand and supply in a free market set-up is essential.
- Over-regulations and over-controls do not pay and must be substituted by normal regulation by professional bodies.
- Monopolies and oligopolies in production and trade have to be replaced, through free entry of new firms, by a competitive economy.
- The private sector of enterprise as well as the NGO sector has to be given larger freedom to invest, expand and perform.
- The public sector enterprises have also to be subjected to structural reform and be given the same freedoms as the private sector firms.
- After receiving these freedoms, if a public enterprise still does not perform well, it could become the subject of what is called disinvestment and, perhaps, handed over to private enterprise.
- The over-valuation of domestic currencies should be corrected and the exchange rate of the national currency should be determined in the market through an interaction of demand and supply and marginal intervention, if necessary, by the Central Bank, but not by the bureaucracy.
- The import of technologies from abroad have to be allowed more freely to generate general goods as well as durable consumer goods for poverty reduction.
- In order to get these technologies a freer flow of foreign capital has to be allowed, perhaps with some consideration for disallowing takeovers and acquisition of local firms, by external parties – at any rate, for an initial period, until a nearly level playing field is established.

In addition to these various recommendations, derived from a distilling of the experience of the economic regimes functioning in the last century and a half – all of them finally impinging on poverty reduction – some more recommendations could be suggested for a speedy removal of the complex poverty phenomenon.

1. In the highly developed market economies – now that peace dividends derived from cuts in nuclear and conventional defence apparatus have been largely absorbed in the civilian economy – the only major method for the conquest of recurring recessions and rising unemployment is trade expansion with the rest of the world. Increasing exports of goods, services and technologies to the rest of the world have become essential, as these will generate employment both at home and in the rest of the world. Developed economies of the first world facing an impasse at home should know that an increase in the purchasing power of the second and the third world is crucial for absorbing the exports from the first world. Technology transfers to the second and third world and rising incomes therein are no longer to be seen as a gift from the first world but a technical necessity for its own prosperity, if not survival.

2. These extra exports from the first world have to be paid for by the second and third world and the only way to get these payments is by exports from the latter to the former. To enable these payments to proceed smoothly, it is important that the industrialized and highly developed countries reduce or eliminate the tariff and non-tariff barriers to their imports from the rest of the world; or else the national debts of the second and third world will increase on the one side and the problems of the developed nations will multiply on the other.

3. Meanwhile, as a reciprocal set of measures, second and third world countries would have to follow anti-inflationary policies, reduce their subsidies and defence expenditures, cut their budget deficits, shun the over-valuation of their currencies, allow freer flow of foreign capital and concentrate on human resource development, management improvement and efficiency orientation. Infrastructure build-up – roads, ports, electric power, communications – and housing expansion provide substantial opportunities for employment and income generation in most countries, especially in the developing economies. Housing, in particular, very much in shortage in most countries, is not just a roof over the head, but also promotes saving, employment, income and aesthetics. It also turns out to be a health-improving and efficiency-enhancing venture. In densely populated countries such as India, it is possible to identify dozens, if not hundreds, of rural pockets in which to lay the

infrastructures of electricity, local roads, sewerage, water supply and municipal facilities (by the state and the private sector) and invite private and public industry to occupy these pockets and build shops, business premises, hospitals, clinics, schools, other social amenities and residential accommodation. These activities will enhance employment, raise the quality of life in rural areas and slow down rural-urban migration which is becoming a great social nuisance. In this scenario, instead of sending people to where infrastructures are, infrastructures will be built where the people are. A healthy urbanization of rural areas will take place, poverty will be removed and the quality of life will improve.

4. A parallel effort in terms of operating training programmes for the jobs demanded by the market will promote human resource development. All these ventures will require a huge flow of capital but the rate of return to this capital ought to exceed the interest to be paid on the capital and a highly productive strategy for economic and social development will have emerged.

HEALTH MEASURES

The following analysis and recommended measures, though elaborated in the context of India – a country with one of the largest populations below the poverty line – are equally applicable to most developing countries.

Increased life expectancy of a population clearly coexists, among other things, with an improvement in the quality of health measures. Even though life expectancy at birth has increased in India quite phenomenally, from about 31 years to 60 years between 1951 and 1991, a long distance has yet to be covered by public and private health promoting organizations. Thousands of primary health centres and sub-centres in India are often like empty shells, though some of them have been working effectively and are probably one of the causes of improved life expectancy. In general, there is widespread absenteeism of doctors, nurses and other health personnel. Thousands of posts remain unfilled and there is a severe shortage of medicines on the shelves. Costs of treatment in the private sector are too high relative to people's income and there is an absence of social health insurance schemes.

In India, only the General Insurance Corporation (GIC) deals with health insurance in a limited way. The GIC is an official organization which has no competition with other health insuring agencies and, hence, the premiums on health policies are very high. Bureaucratic handling of health insurance leads to too many exclusion clauses which prevent effective insurance by excluding this or that disease or ailment. There are many other exclusions on flimsy and irritating grounds. Insurance claims are handled badly and, even when admitted, are awarded too slowly. Moreover, all health insurance so far is for the upper strata of the society, that is to say, confined only to the formal sector, and there is practically none for the informal segments of society.

The need of the moment is to evolve a social health insurance scheme, which will comprehend and include the masses of the relatively poor in societies. As Muneer Alam, R.N. Agarwal and Indrani Gupta (1997) have shown, there is an urgent need to evolve a mechanism for contributions to a Health Care Fund, which could be augmented through the payment of premiums as well as by other means. A kind of cess could be placed on polluting industries and products, which will also augment the fund. These might be the cigarette industry, and the pan-masala, the hard drinks and alcoholic items which pose serious health hazards, as also a cess on road transport services, in particular, the trucks and lorries which are a major atmosphere-polluting health hazard. A large number of corporate businesses which pollute the soil, water and air, can, and ought to be, subjected to a cess to augment the Health Care Fund. This Fund, when invested appropriately, will yield returns which may be fully utilized for health insurance and for augmenting and 'toning up' the health services, including an extensive launch of school health check-up programmes.

The prevention of ever-recurring epidemics is a matter of serious concern as these are great killers *en masse*. While some epidemics of the past have been conquered through public health programmes and public education, new ones are emerging which need to be addressed: tuberculosis, malaria, typhoid, amoebic dysentery and other infectious diseases are also major killers.

It appears that the accumulation of unattended garbage in large quantities in rural as well as urban areas is a potent cause of large-scale morbidity. Strangely enough, while there is substantial attention to personal hygiene, most rural and urban communities do not pay enough attention to community hygiene. The throwing of garbage in and around one's dwelling house, the non-use of dustbins even when they are provided, open drains in the middle of broken roads in the villages, the absence of garbage collection facilities in numerous areas, the severe shortage of water taps, the existence of taps with no running water, and the near-absence of public latrines with adequate cleaning facilities and water supply, all culminate in the propagation of disease. The mountains of decaying and unattended garbage are the breeding grounds of mosquitoes, the focal points where flies, mice and other rodents, cats, dogs and disease-creating insects flourish in great abundance. These polluting centres are spread all over the place. Even in the more organized cities and towns which have established municipalities, it is noticeable that when a road is built or repaired, the contractors go away after laying or repairing it and, typically, leave extensive masses of dirt, broken bricks and decaying materials on both sides, for miles on end. These too become the breeding grounds for vermin. From these living organisms and the heaps of filth and decaying material emerge killer diseases such as malaria, cholera, amoebic dysentry, typhoid, and, through the consequent debilitation of the human body, tuberculosis and other ailments. Perhaps morbidity in countries where these dreadful phenomena exist, can be reduced by a huge percentage, if only garbage collection facilities are organized through public or private agencies, dustbins are provided in large measures, the general public is educated and motivated not to deposit filth and dirt outside the dustbins, road building contractors are penalized for not removing the dirt and decaying material after building a road, public water taps are provided abundantly as a rule, and health campaigns and mechanisms to minimize and eradicate the infectious and contagious diseases are launched on what is termed a war footing.

Despite all the health deficiencies, such improvements that are emerging in municipal facilities and health care measures are leading to an increase in longevity and, in consequence, the age structure of the population even in developing countries is changing in the direction of an abundance of older people in relation to the rest. Several health transitions are in evidence in these countries, such as the dual phenomena of eradication on the one hand, and of an increase on the other in contagious and communicable diseases. There is an outburst of circulatory and heart diseases, an increase in what are called 'rich man's diseases' like diabetes and heart ailments and, indeed, an alarming extension of AIDS which does not distinguish between the rich and the poor.

It is a matter of the highest priority that an educative as well as an operational series of programmes is launched with the firm intention of improving public health and, hence, the efficiency of the working as well as the non-working population. Such efforts must be supported with the deflection of adequate resources for the public as well as the private sector's programmes for the conquest of disease.

ENTITLEMENTS

Amartya Sen (1981) and Jean Dreze (1989) have developed and elaborated the concept of entitlements, which are provided in society through the legal system, the social norms, the property rules and the rights to production and exchange. Entitlements are also provided by modern states through social services and social safety nets such as unemployment allowances, education and health benefits. These economic arrangements as well as the socio-economic status of a person are major determinants of entitlements. The larger the entitlement, the better off economically and socially a person is, and the poorer segments of society, on one ground or another, are generally constrained by very limited entitlements. One of the major objectives of economic and social policy and organization is to enlarge the range of entitlements and the right to entitlement, especially among the downtrodden and ill-provided segments of society.

Sen elaborates his approach to entitlements in several important ways. A person or family may have a right to entitlement by virtue of the property rules of the society, for example the inheritance rules. He may also have a right, again, by legal and social norms, to natural resources such as land, forest and water. Then, his own productive powers such as his ability to give his labour, his capital and natural and other resources in his command, to the process of production, either by working for himself or in an economic or social organization, can augment his entitlement. Moreover, an individual may be able to enlarge his entitlements through his right to exchange what he has and what he produces and, in the process, obtain greater command. Thus, the legal system, the social norms, the productive powers of an individual and his right to exchange, all converge to increase or lower his entitlement. And the objective of greater welfare should certainly be to enlarge the powers of an individual or an organization to obtain greater entitlement. This obviously requires favourable changes in the property rules, the social norms and the productive powers of the society through technological changes and improvement and through greater possibilities for fruitful exchange. In the present situation, individual and institutional environments are highly constrained in most societies and these constraints are a major determinant of widespread poverty.

It is clear that with the adoption of various anti-poverty measures of a micro- and macro-economic nature, from the past and present regimes, as mentioned earlier in this chapter, a major dent will be made in the huge mass of remaining poverty. Thus, poverty will finally be reduced when the following things happen:

(i) when, with market-oriented efficient production of goods and services, mass supplies emerge and with the adoption of appropriate fiscal and monetary policies, the inflation rates slow down;

(ii) when the non-competitive and inefficient firms collapse or merge with the efficient ones, and the efficient ones working on larger scales and up to date technologies, generate large surpluses *en masse* and give much larger employment and entitlements to a well-trained and efficient labour force – thus causing the purchasing power to rise through profits and wage incomes among the masses of the people;

(iii) when mass-produced consumer goods and durable consumer goods are accessed by the poor at affordable prices together with higher employment and higher incomes;

(iv) when, with efficiently managed finance, the private and especially the government (public) sector is able to operate larger entitlements and social safety nets, such as unemployment compensation, old-age pension, social insurance and maternity benefits, partly by charging a price and partly at the state's expense; and

(v) when the renewed and recurring cycles of recessions are conquered through a much better macro-management of the world economies.

Bibliography

Alam, Muneer and Agarwal, R.N. (1997) *Ageing, Macro-Economic Implications and Health Insurance Issues in India – an Exploratory Analysis*

Alam, Muneer and Gupta, Indrani (1997) *Evaluation of the Special School Health Check-up Programme*. NCT of Delhi

Bardhan, Pranab K. (1973) 'On Incidence of Poverty in Rural India in the Sixties', *Economic and Political Weekly*, Vol.8 (Annual Number)

Bardhan, Pranab K. (1984) *The Political Economy of Development*. Oxford, Basil Blackwell

Bhagwati, Jagdish (1993) *India in Transition, Freeing the Economy*. Oxford, Clarendon Press

Bimal, Jalan (1992) *The Indian Economy, Problems and Prospects*. New Delhi, Viking, Penguin India

Blackwood D.I. and Lynch, R.G. (1994) The Measurement of Inequality and Poverty: a Policymaker's Guide to the Literature. *World Development*, 22(4), April 1994, 567–8

Chelliah, Raja J. (1996) 'Towards Sustainable Growth'. Essay in Fiscal and Financial Sector Reforms in India. Delhi, Oxford University Press

Cutler, Peter (1984) 'The Measurement of Poverty: a Review of Attempts to Quantify the Poor, with Special Reference to India', *World Development*, 12(11/12)

Dandekar, V.M. and Rath, N. (1971) *Poverty in India*. Poona, Indian School of Political Economy

Dantwala, M.L. (1973) *Poverty in India, Then and Now* (1870–1970). Delhi, Macmillan

Dhar, P.N. (1990) *Constraints on Growth, Reflections on the Indian Experience*. Delhi, Oxford University Press

Dreze Jean and Sen, A. (1989) *Hunger and Public Action*. Oxford, Clarendon Press

Foster, J. Greer, Joel and Throbecke, A.F. (1984) 'A Class of Decomposable Poverty Measures', *Econometrica*, Vol.52, No.3, 761–6

J. (1984) 'On Economic Poverty: a Survey of Aggregate Measures', in *Advances in Econometrics,* ed. by R.L. Basman and G.F. Rhodes, Vol.3, JAB Press

Foster, J.E. and Sharrocks, A.F. (1991) 'Subgroup Consistent Poverty Indices', *Econometrica*, Vol.59, No.3, May 1991, 687–709

Galbraith, J.K. (1979) *The Nature of Mass Poverty*. Cambridge, Harvard University Press

Govt. of India, Planning Commission (1985) *The Seventh Five Year Plan* (1985–90). New Delhi.

Gupta, S.P. (1995) 'Economic Reform and Its Impact on Poor', *Economic and Political Weekly*, June 3

Haq, Mahbub ul (1995) *Reflections on Human Development*. New York, Oxford University Press

Hashim, S.R. (1996) 'Dimensions of Poverty and Approach to Poverty Alleviation', *Yojna*, Vol.40, No.11

Joshi, P.C. (1979) 'Perspectives on Poverty and Social Change', *Economic and Political Weekly*, Vol.XIV

Khusro, A.M. (1984) *Poverty of Poverty Analysis*, Silver Jubilee Lecture, Delhi, Institute of Economic Growth

Khusro, A.M. (1992) 'Old Order Changeth Yielding Place to New', R.K. Sinha (ed.) *Economic Crisis Management and Challenges*, New Delhi, Deep and Deep Publications

Khusro, A.M. (1992) *TheU-Turn in India's Development Strategies in Recent Development in Economy* (ed. Uma Kapila). Academic Foundation

Khusro, A.M. (1993) *Managing the Indian Economy*. New Delhi, Har Anand Publications

Khusro, A.M. (1994) *Unfinished Agenda: India and the World Economy*. New Delhi, Wiley Eastern Ltd

Krishna, Raj (1980) *Eradicating Mass Poverty*, Seminar, September 1980

Kurien, C.T. (1978) *Poverty, Planning and Social Transformation*. New Delhi, Allied Publishers

Kuznets, Simon (1971) *The Economic Growth of Nations*. Cambridge Mass., Harvard University Press

Minhas, B.S. (1970) Rural Poverty and Distribution and Development Strategy, Facts and Policies, *Indian Economic Review*, Vol.5

Myrdal, Gunar (1968) *Asian Drama: an Enquiry Into the Poverty of Nations*. London, Allen Lane, the Penguin Press, Vol.I, II and III

Nurkse, Ragnar (1953) *Problem of Capital Formation in Under-Developed Countries*. London, Oxford University Press

SAARC (South Asian Association for Regional Cooperation) (1992) *Report of the Independent South Asian Commission on Poverty Alleviation*, Kathmandu ISAC

Sen, Amartya (1976) 'Poverty: an Ordinal Approach to Measurement', *Econometrica*, Vol.44, 219–31

Sen, Amartya (1981) *Poverty and Famines: an Essay on Entitlement and Deprivation*. Oxford, Clarendon Press

Smith, Adam (1934) *An Enquiry into the Nature and Causes of the Wealth of Nations*. London, Methuen, 5th edition

Sukhatme, P.V. (1966) *Feeding India's Growing Billions*. New Delhi, Asia Publishing House

Tendulkar, Suresh D. and Jain, L.R. (1995) Economic Reforms and Poverty, *Economic and Political Weekly*, June 10

UNDP (United Nations Development Programme) (1991) *Human Development Report, 1991*. New York, Oxford University Press

UNDP (1994) *Human Development Report, 1994*. New York, Oxford University Press

UNDP (1995) *Human Development Report, 1995*. New York, Oxford University Press

UNDP (1996) *Human Development Report, 1996*. New York, Oxford University Press

World Bank (1990) *World Development Report, 1990, Poverty*. New York, Oxford University Press

World Bank (1991) *World Development Report, 1991, the Challenge of Development*. New York, Oxford University Press

World Bank (1992) *China Strategies for Reducing Poverty in the 1990s*. Washington, DC World Bank

World Bank (1993) *The East Asian Miracle: Economic Growth and Public Policy: a World Bank Policy Research Report.* New York, Oxford University Press

World Bank (1995) *World Development Report 1995: Workers in a Integrated World.* New York, Oxford University Press

World Bank (1995) *Trends in Developing Economies.* New York, Oxford University Press

World Bank (1995) *Social Indicators of Development.* New York, Oxford University Press

World Bank (1995) *World Tables.* New York, Oxford University Press

World Bank (1995) *India: Country Economic Memorandum – Recent Economic Developments, Achievements and Challenges.* New York, Oxford University Press

Index